BIVVY TRAMPS
A Fenland Carp Tale

by

MARTIN LAWRENCE

ANGLING PUBLICATIONS

First published in 2011

© Copyright Angling Publications Ltd. and Martin Lawrence

British Library Cataloguing in Publication Data

Bivvy Tramps – A Fenland Carp Tale

1. Carp Angling
1. Angling Publications Ltd.

ISBN HB 1-871700-81-7
ISBN SB 1-871700-82-4

Designed and produced by Tim Paisley, Gary Hood and Jemima Musson at Angling Publications Ltd., Regent House, 101, Broadfield Road, Sheffield, S8 0XH.

Cover material supplied by Gary Hood

Cover design by Gary Hood

Printed by MPG Books

Acknowledgements

I would like to thank the many who have contributed to Bivvy Tramps, directly through conversation and advice, and indirectly by their inspiring attitudes and actions. Particular thanks to all those whose words I have quoted to illustrate and embellish the themes and dramatic events of the tale. High fives to Carla Stavrou and Nina Lawrence for reading drafts of the manuscript, pointing out where it needed work, and attention to basic rules of grammar, and apologies for the rules I stubbornly refuse to observe. To all those at Angling Publications who made it happen, I am eternally grateful. Lastly very special thanks to Tim Paisley for his enthusiastic support and belief in the book, his patience and valuable advice and for helping me to realise a lifelong dream. We now hand it over to you, the reader, thanks for buying it!

Dedicated to Phil Shepherd who is largely responsible for my life-long carp fever, the Woolpack boys, a fine bunch of bivvy tramps, and my long suffering family, Nina, Eva and Kai, who have heard 'just going down the lake' far too often.

Part One

I see you stand like greyhounds in the slips,
Straining upon the start. The game's afoot:
Follow your spirit; and upon this charge
Cry 'God for Harry! England, and Saint George!'

William Shakespeare, Henry V, 1599

One

Doubt not that angling is an art. The question is whether you be capable of learning it... he that hopes to be a good angler, must not only bring an enquiring, searching, observing wit, but he must bring a large measure of hope and patience, and a love and propensity to the art itself.

Izaak Walton, 1653

It's too late now, I've publicly promoted myself from camper to carper, which means, no more jumping in the first swim, bargain basement bait, or chuck it and chance it tactics. Definitely no more, that rig will do another session or that boilie still has some life left in it. From now on, a premier league carper, no corners cut, no effort spared. What have I done?

I can hear Tommy pushing out the Zs next door, no doubt dreaming of the Lady. We're on the beach at our local lake, St. Ives Lagoon, my personal Everest. These are my first few tentative steps into the big boys' arena, as until now I've only ever fished the so-called easier lakes on the complex. The Lagoon may not be rock-hard like its neighbour Fen Drayton, or the famous Wraysbury, but it's tough enough to defeat many of the anglers who step up for the challenge.

Gently shelving banks support a thin line of budding willows, and fresh green reeds shooting through last year's brown and battered debris. Two large wooded islands break up its thirty acres and provide some immediately obvious spots to target. It's a mature gravel pit, not unpleasing to the eye, but scarred by the new Cambridge guided bus car park. This morning it's largely empty, Sunday providing a welcome respite from the cars, thundering gravel lorries and pounding rock crushers that pollute its tranquillity six days a week. This is a fishing heaven best enjoyed by anglers hard of hearing, wearing an iPod, or, failing that, a good pair of earplugs!

Living in St. Ives it's hard to focus on any other carp than her ladyship, but I've only seen her once. It's hard to believe a fish that big can be so elusive. Last summer, while strolling around on a glorious midweek morning, Tommy and I found her basking in the top bay. Tommy sprinted to the beach swim, grabbed his stalking rod, and galloped back, anxious that someone else may notice her. It was an awesome sight, like a *sunken rowing boat*, to borrow Yates's famous phrase. A couple of frustrating hours were spent trying to tempt her, but she just wasn't having it and eventually one too many floaters dragged into her path ruined the chance. She drifted out towards the islands and I've not seen her since.

Anglers come from across the country to tempt her, cars crammed with carp catching kit. Pungent aromas wafting from the latest delicacies of ingenious carp chefs. Thousands of pounds and hundreds of hours spent creating the perfect strategy to crack the Lagoon. *The Lady is mine!* Laying awake visualising the moment of success, pulling the net over her fulsome curves, cradling her in their arms. Straining and staring intensely for the trophy shot! The Fat Lady is the biggest in the Lagoon by some distance, hovering around an impressive 60lb. Her fabulous lips, wide grey back, and enormous belly make her a top target. Fat Lady may look like a bit of a porker, but the boys admire her curves, and size definitely matters. One of the biggest carp in England, she's a real Fenland jewel, a national treasure. Sadly, as yet, she's not one of the notches on my bedchair.

Stepping from their cars you can almost see the confidence draining from Lagoon virgins. A glazed look, like bunnies in headlights. Over the top and into the arena, are they really up to it? Were they really onto something, or was it just wishful thinking? No turning back now. Load up the barrow and let the games begin. An hour, a day, a month later and the Lagoon still shields its scaly treasures from these earnest campers. Clutching at windswept straws and their pet plans they head for favourite swims. Ahead lies the comforting ritual of *'just setting up mate'*. Rods, pods, bivvies and bait. Marker rod, spod rod: baits cast, lines sunk, bobbins hung, traps set. Sit back, brew up. Watch and Wait. A time for reflection! *Did I hit the mark? Did I move the lead? Are the rigs sitting right?* Raking over every detail. Hook size, hooklink and Hair length, lead size, type and colour, fixed or running, and on and on. *Am I fishing or camping?* If you're faking it the Lagoon will find you out. You can sit there all year, but unless you're the real deal, you might as well reel in, sit back and enjoy the scenery, you're a CAMPER!

"Quack, quack-quack."

"Morning Kes, anything to report?"

"Nothing, except the old fella is coming for a cuppa."

"I heard that, you cheeky pup," Ron says coming round the corner, stalking rod in hand.

"Sorry Ron, only joking," I say.

"You better be. Anyway, why are you both round here when her ladyship is head-down in By-pass bay?"

Ron is a method man: location, location, location. He won't put a rod in the water until he's seen a fish, and has been known to spend whole days, walking, talking, sitting and staring. I like to wind him up.

"You'll catch bugger-all with your rods in the car Ron."

"You may be a chuck it and chance it merchant Kes, but I'm not. As Cloughie used to say, it only takes a second to score a goal. Give me half an hour on the fish and I'll nick one."

He quite often does!

"There she is boys," Ron whispers. A huge dark grey tail wafts in the weeds, about four rod lengths out.

"That's her alright," Tommy says, pulling off his Fox fleece and running a hand through his cropped grey hair.

"This is a monster, monster chance, and it's your honour Ron."

"I know, I'm shitting myself! My hands are shaking so much I can hardly thread the maggots on."

Ron flicks out his size 8 hook loaded with wrigglers just beyond the Lady. The small Drennan crystal float lays flat on the surface, and his 12lb X-line slips away at a pleasing angle. The maggots squirm appetisingly a couple of feet in front of her leathery lips.

"Boys, is my float moving or am I imagining it?"

"It's going mate, wait for it, could be a liner," Tommy says.

Slowly the float glides across the surface and the line tightens. Ron steadies himself and then sweeps back his Daiwa Infinity.

Later, back in the shop, none of us says much. I busy myself with stocking the racks, iPod blasting metal into my skull. Ron sits out the back, bagging up our special Lagoon spod mix. Tommy comes over and waves his hands in front of my face. "Turn that bloody racket down!"

"Can you hear it?" I shout.

Tommy pulls out one of the earplugs. "You'll be deaf by the time you're thirty you know."

"Good, I won't have to listen to you nagging any more."

Tommy gives me a slap on the back of the head. "Cheeky little sod. I've decided we need a tonic for the troops."

"Boomtown Rats, 1978," Ron shouts, a small smile flicking across his face.

"That's the spirit Ron, you'll get another crack at her. She wouldn't be worth having if she was too willing. Let's shut up shop for half an hour and I'll buy us all a nice fry-up at the café."

No matter what mental torture the Lagoon has dished out that day, we all enjoy breakfasts at Joe's café. St. Ives soul food comes in the shape of black pudding, mushrooms, bacon, eggs and beans.

And so it goes!

Two

*A man who habitually fishes for carp has a strange look in his eyes.
I have known and have shaken hands respectfully with the man who
caught the biggest carp in England. He looked as if he had been in
heaven and in hell and had nothing to hope from life.*

Arthur Ransome, 1929

Welcome to my world, the Ouse valley. We don't really do hills round here, but what the landscape lacks in height it makes up in depth. Fishing heaven round every corner, and St. Ives is no exception. Tommy's Tackle, just off Market Hill (must be a joke!), is at the hub of this angling nirvana. In the summer months we get trade from the passing boats, mostly maggots, floats, and hooks. Boat anglers are easy to spot, it's a 'boiled lobster in deck shoes and shorts' look. But the boat brigade are light entertainment, an aside from the main business of serving our small dedicated gaggle of match men and the khaki-clad carpers.

Take a peak at the back cover of Jack Hilton's book *Quest for Carp* and you'll see my home village, Hemingford Grey, boasted some of the biggest carp in England back in the '60s. Today it's the same story all the way along the Ouse Valley, lake after lake, all with the potential to throw up a lump. And don't forget the glorious Ouse itself, winding through the willows and meadows of Cambridgeshire, home to unknown hard-fighting commons and lost residents of syndicates. Even our glorious Fat Lady has done some time in the river, liberated for a few months by one of the spectacular winter floods we get out here. For those dedicated few, who aren't afraid of a long walk, the river offers a last frontier of English carp fishing.

So, where better than St. Ives for a carp fishers' emporium? Well, you'd have thought so. Trouble is, Tommy refuses to embrace the online shopping revolution. His dad started the shop in 1977 and Tommy has hardly changed a thing since he took over ten years ago. He's even put an Internet swear box on the counter. It's like Lord Voldemort from Harry Potter, the thing that cannot be spoken. Any of the regulars who mention it in his presence have to donate 50p to Save the Children. Last month we sent them £20, and if we're not careful it could become the most successful part of the business. My latest mission is to turn Tommy into an *ebay* enthusiast and save Ron and me from getting the boot.

Sorry, drifted off into Mr Gloomy land, which is not the way I wanted to start at all. Working at Tommy's is brilliant. I get to talk about carp fishing all day long five days a week, and in between I go carp fishing. What more could you want from life? I've been cycling down London Road and over the medieval bridge to get maggots since I was eight years old. The second that pungent mix of ammonia from the maggots and myriad boilie flavours wafts up my hooter I feel at home. It's not the most modern of tackle shops; in fact, some might say it's a poky little cave. We can't display bivvies, bedchairs and other big items, so focus on bait and the rig boards, which are always fully loaded with the latest paraphernalia. Most of which, in my opinion – although Tommy has banned me from discussing this in the shop – is more about catching anglers than it is about catching carp.

When it's quiet, we kill time taking the piss out of each other's top five this or that. Today it's top five carp anglers of all time. I put Terry Hearn at number one, while Tommy goes for Peter Springate, closely followed by Rod Hutchinson. Ron is still staring thoughtfully at his list.

"Come on then Ron, let's have it." I say. "We know we can always expect something bizarre from Ron."

"Old Git' Simmons."

"Well, you ignorant bastards may think it all started in the 1970s, but you're well off the mark. The pioneer of modern carp fishing was Otto Overbeck. He was camouflaging his lines, prebaiting, mixing up specials way back in 1908, not to mention catching quite a few lumps, so I reckon he deserves top spot."

"Otto bleedin' Overbeck, are you off your trolley Ron? Hey Tommy, did you hear that? I'm surprised he didn't have Izaak Walton in there. Oh no, he did, look he's crossed him out."

"Piss off Kes, you said top five of *all time*, so Walton must be in with a shout. And what's more, I bet neither of you included the Billing wizard, Bob Reynolds."

"OK Ron, fair play, Bob Reynolds is a connoisseur's choice," Tommy says.

"Old farts' choice more like," I say.

Tommy pins up the lists behind the counter thinking it will be amusing to see the reaction from our regulars.

Top five carp anglers

Tommy	Kes	Ron
Peter Springate	Terry Hearn	Otto Overbeck
Rod Hutchinson	Dave Lane	Rod Hutchinson
Kevin Maddocks	Peter Springate	Chris Yates
Jack Hilton	Jim Shelley	Richard Walker
Terry Hearn	Lee Jackson	Bob Reynolds

The Post Office made Ron redundant five years ago. It knocked him for six. He was fifty then and really struggled to find any regular work. He tried doing nights at Tesco, but it didn't suit him, he was so used to being outside doing his round. Ron was spending so much time in the shop, drinking tea, chatting to customers and helping out that Tommy offered him a job. It was only part-time, but he seemed thrilled, and Tommy's never regretted it. Ron's rock-solid, dependable and comfortingly, built like a bull mastiff.

According to Tommy, Ron and I are better salesmen than anglers, which on current results is certainly true. Ron is patient and enthusiastic; he sells people tackle they didn't know they wanted. Years of angling experience have taught him to understand what they need. His hands glide over the rig racks, picking a packet here and there, hinting at the possibilities. Before they know it they are tapping in their PIN, having bought a stack of tackle, convinced it's what they had in mind. I, on the other hand, like to steam roller customers into a purchase. "I can't believe you don't own Korda Underwater series part V. It will change your life mate!" They buy it. "You mean you haven't tried these maggot clips?" Out come the ten-pound notes.

Tommy has put me in charge of the second-hand book bin. It's full of general coarse fishing books that I buy down the boot sale or in the local charity shops. To be honest, although I'm a massive enthusiast for any kind of fishing book, it seems I'm more of an anorak about this than most of our customers. The stock turnover is depressingly slow. To liven it up we've taken to making bets on which one will sell next. Take the other day: I had a £5.00 wager with Ron and Tommy that "Go fishing with Jack Charlton" would be the next book to sell. Now Jack Charlton is royalty, an English World Cup winner, and out of respect we keep it priced at £4.99, which I have to admit is pretty expensive for what is, and I hate to say this about a national hero, not the most compelling of books. Anyway, last week a chap came in wearing a replica 66 shirt, his bald head closely matching it. "Boat brigade ahoy," Ron whispered. Casually browsing through the book box, he found Jack. His body language changed, holding it up like a trophy, flicking through slowly and reverently like it's a first edition of 'Stillwater Angling'. After a nail-biting couple of minutes, he rushed over, whacked a fiver down on the counter and promptly left. Get in there, that's £2.50 each you owe me boys. We all miss Jack, but feel proud having held out on the price.

Three

My comfort was a blanket and a groundsheet. My equipment: an optimistic four sacks, a length of rope, a tin of hooks, a nine foot, three pound test curve glass rod and a Mitchell Mer reel loaded with eleven pound line, a home-made bite alarm and a home-made landing net.

Bob Reynolds, on his Billing captures from 1957

I've recently inherited the Kingfisher, a 45ft narrowboat. It was dad's pride and joy but mum was never that into it, so here I am, with my very own home, moored up in St. Ives' Boathaven. Still feels a bit weird though; the whole place has dad written all over it. It's not your typical Rosie and Jim narrowboat, with plants on the roof and floral patterned soft furnishings. Dad applied his modern male taste of dark blue sides, white roof, and white trim. Not a swirl or bloom in sight. Inside the whole place is finished in light oak, with plain dark blue curtains, cushions and carpets. And talk about spick and span; every surface was buffed to the edge of destruction. When I moved in you could eat your dinner off the floor. Bits of kit stowed in the endless custom storage cupboards dad had the poor boat builder install. Dad knew where everything belonged. I on the other hand have spent the first few weeks scrabbling around opening and closing doors trying to bloody find this and bloody that. In fact, I've given up. As I lie here in my bunk, I can see bits and bobs scattered around the cabin, in a Kes-style accessible open storage system. Dad would not have approved. "A tidy tackle box comes from a tidy mind," he would say every time he saw my jumbled mess.

He would have been particularly freaked by the conversion of his lounge area into a fishing store. I spent yesterday afternoon going through my gear assessing its potential for a newly promoted carper. I've got dad's tackle back at mum's, but to be honest, it's pretty old, and not what people are using down the Lagoon these days. From what I've seen ultra-cult carpers have a head full of knowledge and a car full of kit. The former you can only get through experience, but I can do something about the kit. So, is my tackle up to the job? Well I've had no complaints so far. But seriously, my trusty old Daiwa Powermesh rods are so 1990s, pretty knackered and a bit lightweight for fishing the islands. I've got my eye on a set of 3lb Free Spirits. All I can say is, these wands are the nuts! I would ask Tommy to get me some through the shop, but to be honest I can't really afford even a discounted new set of the Hi-S range, and he's so strapped for cash at the moment I don't like to bother him with favours right now. I'll be looking out for a second-hand steal on *ebay*.

Also on the *ebay* watch list are new reels. It's still hard to beat the Shimano Baitrunners for close to medium range, but they're not the ones for hitting long-range marks. I really fancy a set of *Daiwa SS3000s* or their *Tournament 5000Ts*. Trouble is, the basic kit for a Lagoon campaign doesn't come cheap, even if you're hunting on *ebay* for the deals of the decade. You need a bit of wedge to look the part on the Lagoon; not that I'm a tackle tart at heart, it's just I don't want to look obviously out of my depth. I reckon £300 minimum for three decent used rods, £400 on reels, line £100, another £200 on bits and bobs for the tackle box, and £350 for the right to fish. Somehow I'm going to have to find around £1500 to get myself all the tools for the job.

And there's more pain! My scales only weigh up to 30lb and a 32 inch landing net is clearly not big enough to serve the Lady. She'll need a bigger bankside bed than my meagre 40cm x 80cm mat, so I've got my eye on one of those monster JRC carp cots. The most embarrassing item is my brolly, which has been in the rod bag since I was eight. It has bits of tape and stitched repairs all over it. Two of the spokes are broken, the pole no longer extends, and, crucially, it leaks like a sieve. It'll have to go! On a more positive note, while not the current fashion, my Fox Stalker rod pod is pretty good, and EOS buzzers do the job. I'd really like a set of Neville's and Matrix stainless bank sticks, but I've got to be sensible, for now at least. A Nash Titan bivvy and Fox Ultra bedchair are my best bits of kit, which probably says a lot about my priorities. You know what growing lads are like, we love our kip!

No lying in bed this morning though, it's 7.00 a.m., time for my weekly pilgrimage to Crystal Lakes car boot sale on the road to Fenstanton. You could say I'm a bit obsessive, fanatical, a fundamentalist when it comes to the art of car booting. Like fishing, there are plenty of blank days when the field is full of junk, but the lure of rare carpy treasure brings me back religiously week after week. Not coming would be like not playing your lottery numbers the very time they come up. Too painful to risk! So every Sunday I sacrifice a bit of bite time, reel in and head off across the field to my other happy hunting ground.

The place is already packed when I arrive. I park my battered red Passat estate and hurry over to the long line of cars, feeling anxious that others will have already nabbed the best bargains. The first ten or so pitches have an uninspiring mix of baby kit, old clothes, videos and general tat. But just when I'm thinking I've been overly optimistic I come across a fantastic sight, a whole stall of tackle. On closer inspection I decide it's mostly cheap Chinese rubbish, but there are one or two interesting pieces.

"How much do you want for the big mat mate?" I ask.

"£18," he barks in a gruff Scottish accent.

I'm interested, a good price, but try my luck. "Would you take £15?"

"Nah, can't do it pal. I sell 'em all day long in the shop for £28. I've knocked off a tenner already."

This must be bullshit. Why would he be at a Sunday morning boot sale if his shop was doing a roaring business Monday to Friday? Anyway, aren't you supposed to haggle a bit at boot sales? As there are four monster mats on the stall I decide to move on, and maybe come back later.

Time for a cup of tea and a bacon roll, but hang on, what's that? I notice a rod leaning against a car in the corner of the field. Breakfast will have to wait. I arrive a little too enthusiastically, which can ruin your bargaining power. Best not to look too keen.

"Morning mate, all reasonable offers considered," says the lad on the stall, looking every inch a hardcore carper in his Carpe Diem hoodie and Fox cap.

"How much for the Nash scales?" I ask as casually as I can muster.

"Well the dial is cracked, but they still work. A tenner to you. They'll do for any carp in England."

"Cool, I'll take them. Hopefully they'll be weighing the Black Pig and the Fat Lady some time this year," I say.

"Nice fish, but it's a bit too busy down there for me. I've been over on Ron Middleton's water at Earith, the Ashmire syndicate. Lovely water, cracking fish and very quiet."

"Yeah sounds good, bit pricey though isn't it?" I say

"Not at all, three hundred notes well spent in my book. I'm looking for somewhere bigger now though and have my eye on Fen Drayton. Fancy that linear Jim Shelley caught a few years back."

"Oh yeah, I saw that on the CarpForum, 48lb wasn't it?" I say.

"That's right, an absolute stunner, and totally unknown at the time. They reckon she has a few bigger mates too."

"I don't think I'm ready for the Fen yet."

"I know what you mean; over 90 acres of water can be just a little bit daunting at the best of times."

"I'm Kes by the way."

"Pleased to meet a fellow addict Kes, I'm Steve," he says giving me a bone crushing handshake.

I instantly warm to this guy, bursting with enthusiasm and friendly with it. A true brother of the angle!

"Here you are Kes, this is what you need for the Lady," Steve says holding up a really nice Trakker weighsling.

"How much?"

"Well seeing as it's going to a good home and for a good cause, a fiver."

"Cheers Steve, it's a deal."

I am well pleased with my morning's haul, but decide to have one more crack at the mat.

"Me again, I can't leave it alone," I say.

"The price is still eighteen quid," the man replies.

"You won't move at all?"

"Sorry pal, people have been taking the piss all morning. I've just about had it right now."

"OK, how about £17?" I venture, smiling.

"Right, seeing as you want to haggle, £17.99 is my best price."

"Go on then, you're right it's a good price, £17.99 it is."

Handing over £18 I tell him to keep the change, and make a hasty exit.

Four

*So far as my experience goes, it is certain that good luck is the most
vital part of the equipment of him who would seek to slay big carp.
For some men I admit the usefulness of skill and pertinacity; for
myself I take my stand entirely on luck.*

H T Sheringham, 1911

"Have you seen this piece in the local rag, about how fishing is next in line
now that fox hunting is banned," Ron barks, leaning on the counter.

"Yeah I did, it's about Jay Johnson, lead singer of The Bunnyhuggers. I
went to school with him," I say.

"Bunnyhuggers, says it all doesn't it!"

"They've formed a protest group called *FishAction*."

"Ruddy marvellous, that's all I need, animal rights protesters camped outside the
shop," Tommy says, "business is bad enough with the poxy Internet."

"A close encounter with my priest will make him think twice," Ron says.

"Ok chaps, enough of this doom and gloom. Time for another top five," Tommy
says.

"What, top five ways to cook a Bunnyhugger?" Ron says.

"No, but I thought we might actually do one that's not fishing related for a change."

"Err, why?" I ask.

"Bloody hell, you two can be hard work sometimes. You'll enjoy this: give me your
best band and best album of all time," Tommy says.

He's right, we're all into our music and so a focused calm descends as we peruse our
musical memories while stocking bait onto the shelves.

"I'll make us a nice brew and then we'll do it," Tommy says as he descends into hell,
otherwise known as Tommy's Tackle storeroom.

Apart from being a bivvy tramp, I'm also a major metal head. My current musical
heroes are Jim Root, aka #4, from Slipknot, and Jack White. Dad was a total heavy rock

man, so I'm well into Jimmy Page, Ritchie Blackmore and Angus Young, too. I first picked up the guitar when I was seven, and had 'Back in Black' and 'Smoke on the Water' down by the age of ten. I'm pretty much either thinking about carp or guitars. Well, girls too I suppose. Yeah, sex, beer, metal and fishing, that's all there is, right? Ron's mind is considerably further back in time. In the '60s, decked out in Ben Sherman shirt, sharp suit and parka he was an avid Kinks and Who fan, then in the late '70s it was The Jam, Elvis Costello and northern soul.

"Right Ron. Let me guess. The Who, ' Meaty Beaty Big and Bouncy'."

"It was up there Tommy, but no, without doubt, the best band of all time, who did it all and better than most were The Beatles."

"A bit bloody obvious Ron; I thought you were mod and new wave through and through, not a mop top!" Tommy says.

"Well I am, but credit where it's due, just look at their list of great albums, and topping that list for me is the majestic Revolver."

"Your turn Kes," Tommy says.

"I'm running free yeah, I'm running free!" I belt out with gusto.

"You're having a laugh, Iron Maiden, best band of all time?"

"No, best album, 'Prowler', 'Running Free', 'Transylvania', 'Iron Maiden', and 'Charlotte the Harlot', classics from beginning to end. I'm going for their first album from1980, a belter then and now, and one of the first true metal albums."

"Iron Maiden my ARSE!" chips in Ron. "So who's your best band then? Let me guess, Metallica."

"Good call, but no, 'Back in Black', 'Hell Ain't a Bad Place To Be', 'Highway to Hell', and '42, 39, 56 you could say she's got it all'.... 'Whole Lotta Rosie', it's got to be..."

"AC bloody DC," says Ron. "Right, you're up next Tommy, and I can just feel what's coming; more high voltage long hair noise."

"Too right, Ron. England's finest are about to make their way into Tommy's Tackle Hall of Rock 'N' Roll fame. And fighting for top spot on the proprietor's best band of all time list are, Blackmore's awesome creative team, Deep Purple, the legendary foursome that is Led Zeppelin and our local heroes Pink Floyd. And the winners are – the mighty Floyd!"

"Good choice Tommy; so what's the best album then, 'Ummagumma'?" I ask.

"Yeah, OK, but maybe not their best. No, the best album of all time, and also the best live album of all time, is *Live and Dangerous*."

"Thin feckin' Lizzy. What did I do to deserve this life, wall to wall bloody long hairs?" Ron moans.

"Nice one Tommy, quality riffery and the Irish legend that is Mr Phil Lynott," I say.

"Thank you folks, that concludes our awards ceremony, the results will be posted shortly on the door of the bait fridge. Thanks for coming and have a safe journey home," Tommy announces, to an empty shop.

"So when are we going to get our ears blasted by *Radiation* again; about time you got back out there isn't it?" Ron asks.

"Yeah, probably, heart's not in it at the moment. Once the carp come out to play, I just want to be on the bank," I say.

"I thought you had some interest from a record label?"

"Yeah, there's always talk, mostly from us, and not a lot of action."

"You don't want to get stuck in here with us your whole life Kes. Besides, if things don't look up I can't see much future for the shop," Tommy says.

"I could think of far worse places to be."

"And I could think of plenty a lot better. Have you been down to Huntingdon Tackle? It's like a bloody supermarket. Rob must be raking it in!"

"Rubbish, you love it here," I say.

"I'd love it a lot more if it paid the bills, and some."

"I keep telling you, we should be flogging stuff on *ebay*."

"Hey, that's 50p in the swear box thank you very much."

"At least let me show you what's on there; I bet you've never looked."

"Right, here's an idea; you've got five minutes to sell it to me, like that programme Dragon's Den," Tommy says, "but remember I've got a short fuse about this stuff!"

I fire up the laptop, hit my *ebay* shortcut on the desktop, and type in 'carp fishing tackle'.

"Look here Tommy, page after page of tackle. Someone's flogging a Fox Stalker rod pod. Six bids, 15 minutes left and it's at £45."

"Not much of a margin is it? We sell them for £65," Tommy replies.

"Yeah, but we've had ten downstairs for months! Better to sell them for £50. And it doesn't cost us anything to post, 'cos that's listed separately. I'll pack items up when we're quiet and take them up the Post Office."

"Bet they take a fair old wedge out of the profit?"

"It's not too bad, a few pence to list an item in an auction and then about ten percent of the sale price. We can even have an online shop."

"Ten percent, cheeky buggers?"

"It's no different to a normal auction house, and your market on *ebay* is massive."

"I suppose so," Tommy says grudgingly.

"Must cost a fortune setting it all up, getting the web pages sorted and what have you?"

"No it's really easy, I can do all that. I buy and flog stuff on *ebay* all the time. You'll love this: let me show you the carp books' auction."

"Well there you go; somebody's selling a signed copy of 'Carp Fever' for £15. That's just extracting the Michael," Tommy says.

"It's the starting price, to draw people in. He'll have a reserve and it'll creep up over the next few days, then go mad in the last hour. Wouldn't be surprised if it made a hundred quid."

"Well that's a bit more respectable: carp fishing history, that is!" Tommy says.

I browse through a few more items, trying to sell the idea to this sceptical dragon.

"What do you think?" I ask.

"Well, I don't know Kes, it's alright but sounds like a lot of faffing about, getting cheques off people and backwards and forwards to the Post Office."

"You don't use cheques Tommy. They pay it straight to you via something called PayPal. It goes into your account electronically. It's brilliant!"

"Oh blimey, I don't like the sound of that; Internet banking, I've heard bad things about that."

"Come on Tommy, things have moved on, even I know that. Give Kes a chance to try it," Ron says.

Tommy looks at Ron sceptically, "I'm not promising anything, but tell you what, let's pick a few items and see how they do."

Soon it's five o'clock and we're locking up the shop after another day full of banter, but no sales. Outside a chilly easterly is racing up the High Street. I pull my Carpworld hoodie down against the rain and hurry through the early evening shoppers towards the pub. Tommy and Ron head off for a night on the Lagoon. A welcoming warm beery fug hits me. I take a long drag and head for the line of real ale pumps. The Royal Tavern is a proper old boozer with snugs and bars spread out along a wood-panelled passage. Pint in hand I wander down to the wonderfully dark and seedy band room at the end, the walls covered with classic rock band posters, the lino floor sticky from spilt pints. In the corner is a small stage and enough space for a hundred people to crush in and mosh it up. If Tommy's Tackle is my second home then this is a close third. Every last Thursday of the month *Radiation* can usually be heard belting out our own brand of nasty metal to a small but loyal following of fen head bangers. Tonight the room is quiet and almost empty, save for a couple tucked away in the snug.

"Hello Kes," calls a familiar voice from the corner. It's Jay, a lad who was in my year at school, and his girlfriend Saira. She was a couple of years younger than us, and a total pain in the arse. On the plus side she's tall and blond, with blue eyes. They both think they're pretty cool, Saira in her black jeggings, black mini skirt, and red T-shirt, Jay with his stupid black dinner jacket and Smiths T-shirt. How the hell Jay managed to hook up with her I don't know, he's such a short arse, with crazy curly ginger hair. He was so square at school, but he's gone all Q magazine now, with his big earrings, ripped jeans and Converse trainers.

"Alright, checking out the venue eh; I saw you on the gig list."

"Yeah, bit of a dump isn't it?"

"Hey, watch it, this is holy ground."

"More like Hell. What do you reckon the regulars will make of The Bunnyhuggers?"

"Probably sling you on the barbie out the back."

"Very funny," Saira says, legs crossed, bouncing a large Doc Marten up and down, "you still tormenting those poor fish?"

"No not really, haven't caught one for about six months."

"Good. I can't understand what you see in it. You don't even eat them. I could almost understand it if you ate them, but just yanking them out and slinging them back is sadistic."

"Look we've had this discussion so many times. We'll just have to agree to disagree. In the spectrum of cruel acts, it's not up there with chopping shark fins off and putting them back in the sea, or clubbing baby seals to death for their fur."

"Doesn't justify it in my view."

"Too right Jay, all anglers should be chucked in a lake and dragged round by their lips. See how they like it," Saira says.

"Lovely; who's the sadist? Can we change the subject?" I say, regretting my decision to wander down here.

"Have you heard? We've got a new drummer, Jane Boston; she's pretty hardcore." Jay says.

"She's the one who chained herself to the tree by the river when they were doing the flood defences," I say.

"That's right. The bastards nearly killed her, chainsawing and bulldozing the tree she was camped in."

"Well, she's got guts, I'll give her that. I was pissed off when they cut those trees down. The meadow looks grim without them."

"Glad we can agree on that," Jay says. "Anyway, are you coming on Saturday, to hear what a real rock band sounds like?"

"Doubt it. I'll be camped up on the Lagoon."

"I'd recommend selling your gear while you've got the chance. You won't get much for it once the ban comes," Saira says.

"You won't leave it alone will you. I read about this new group you've started. Let's just say that if some loony government banned fishing, I'd be straight on the Chunnel to France, with my fishing gear."

"You in France, that's a laugh. They wouldn't let you into Essex let alone France."

"I don't know where you get them from Saira, but I have to hand it to you, it's a bottomless pit."

Saira bows her head, and gives me the customary middle finger.

"Nice!" I say.

"Well, don't forget we're protesting at the fishing match on Sunday morning. Why don't you join us? Bring a rock to chuck in," Jay says.

"Not top of my list of things to do on a Sunday morning, but I'll bear it in mind."

My nerves are jangling after the encounter with Saira. I know Jay is just as committed to animal rights, but somehow he doesn't seem as venomous, and I'm not really up for dealing with it lately. I head for the Lagoon to cadge a brew off Ron or Tommy. Dad keeps popping into my mind, particularly when thinking about fishing. He loved '*Apocalypse Now*' and would strut around his swim like Robert Duvall's character shouting "I love the smell of Monster crab in the morning... smells like... VICTORY!" and "You gonna fish boy, cos Kooks don't fish do they?" I'd lie in my sleeping bag laughing my head off.

The wind is howling into Waitrose Bay, and tucked into the reeds I can see Ron's bivvy flexing in the wind, his three Daiwa Infinitys being hammered by huge waves.

"Any good Ron?"

"Nothing mate. Could be a messy night. Fancy a brew?"

"You star Ron, must have read my mind."

"You all right? You look a bit pale!"

"Oh I'm fine. Just a bit tired, what with everything that's happened lately, and still cracking on with the band. Could do with a few days chilling on the Lagoon."

"You know she hasn't been out for a few months. Maybe you should ask Tommy for a couple of days off next week."

"Yeah maybe, where's Tommy?"

"He's on the old lake. The lazy bastard couldn't be bothered to carry his gear down here. I think he's only here for the evening."

At that moment Ron's phone rings. I hear Tommy shriek, "I'm in Ron, feels big!"

"You jammy bastard!" Ron shouts.

We look at each other in disbelief: fish on, first one in months. "Come on Ron, let's get up there and watch the action," I say

"Nah, you go; I just spent ages getting my rods on the spots."

"Don't be an arse! How many times do we get to see Tommy play a Lagoon carp?"

Ron hauls in his rods, and we charge along the Car Park bank.

When we get there Tommy is standing in the lake up to his waist, rod parallel to the water, line ripping from his Shimano.

"Where is it Tommy?" I ask, peering into the descending gloom.

"It's right on the edge of the island, trying to get round the back. I had it on the left, and it bombed along the tree line, bow waving all the way."

This is a tense time; something to be enjoyed, but in the back of all our minds is the gut-wrenching thought that so much could go wrong and the rod ping back limp and lifeless. Tommy is joined in battle with a Lagoon monster, determined to use all his 30 years of experience and skill to transform this grey damp June evening into a glorious golden memory. The carp is equally focused on escaping the unseen danger, marshalling every ounce of power and speed to escape into the weedy depths.

"Do you think it's her?" Ron asks.

"Shut up, I don't want to think about it."

"It's on the top Tommy," I say, perched in a willow.

A big splash reveals the fish has made it into the channel between the islands.

"Oh no, here we go again." Tommy's rod slams down and his line glances against branches hanging down from the old lake island. "You've got to wade further to the right Tommy, I'll go along and see if I can lob a rock beyond her."

"OK, good idea."

Tommy's line is singing in the wind, and he can feel the butt bending. The fish is close to breaking free. A hefty rock plunges into the depths, just beyond the boil in the water. Instinctively it bolts away, and the pressure is gone. Sensing freedom it powers on gathering speed, picking its way between the weedbeds. The line goes slack.

"Oh shit, shit, shit, it's come off," Tommy cries, winding and pumping the rod furiously, his 17lb X-line racing through the water, the Infinity bending into battle curve as he contacts the fish again.

"It's still on," Tommy shouts.

The line cuts across the fish's face and up its flank, clipping the dorsal fin. Tommy can feel every vibration, each time thinking it's over. The fish is exhausted, its runs becoming shorter and slower. Tommy senses his chance and piles on the pressure. Beaten, it rolls on the surface, belly up, and he draws the great prize toward the waiting net, Ron crouching low, concentrating hard. In one swift movement, it's ours.

"Come on you beauty!" Tommy shouts.

"Congratulations mate, it's a big 'un," I say.

"It's the Pig!" Tommy says, "A new one for me, YES!"

"You the man, Tommy, you the man!" I say, exchanging high fives.

"Have you got golden balls or what Mr Tindall?" Ron says, galumphing down into the swim and slapping Tommy on the back.

"What, you think it was lucky? Pure skill, and years and years of watercraft went into that one."

"Watercraft my arse," Ron says, "you just plonked yourself in there 'cos it did a bite last weekend and you didn't fancy trekking right round to where the fish are."

"Oh yeah!" Tommy says.

"The fish are clearly down your end Ron, that's why Tommy blanked his arse off, NOT," I say laughing. Ron gives Tommy a few friendly jabs in the ribs, enjoying his friend's success. It may have been a lucky capture, but they all count.

Tommy gets his scales and weighsling. We all stare down in awe at the huge frame of the Black Pig, deep grey flank, rounded back, drop belly, mouth slowly pulsing, sucking for oxygen after its valiant fight.

"Give me a hand to lift her Ron."

The needle slowly creeps round the dial; 20, 30, 40, 43lb 12oz.

"What a kipper!" I say, firing up my Nikon D50.

"Monster!" Ron shouts.

Five

*And your paste must be thus made: take the flesh of a rabbit
or a cat cut small, and bean flour, and then mix these
together, and put to them either sugar or honey.*

Izaak Walton, 1653

Seeing the Black Pig last night has given me a wake up call: got to get my arse in gear, so I'm lying in bed thinking about bait choice for a Lagoon campaign. Before any action, I always prefer to lie down and think; more haste less speed and all that. Anyway, as you can see from this quote, an obsession with HNV specials has been going on for quite some time: even our Lord Izaak was up to some strange old practices in pursuit of an edge in the bait department. There are people who believe in the holy grail of an ultimate bait. I'm not one of them. At the risk of being controversial, I have to say there's more rubbish written about bait than any other aspect of carp fishing. No, hang on a minute, maybe it's rigs... Well let's settle for agreeing there's a lot of rubbish written about bait and rigs. Actually bait is another subject I'm banned from talking about in the shop. It gets right up my nose every time the bait company reps come round and tell us about the amazing results they're getting with the latest boilie recipe, expecting us to lap it up. And I can't stand 'celebrity' anglers writing articles about how they caught 20 thirties and a couple of forties in a night while using it. I suppose if we stopped buying so much of the latest wonder recipe, we wouldn't be fed a constant stream of new versions.

I'm not saying some of the bait isn't good at catching carp, but what I've learnt from Ron, Tommy and dad is that a good quality food bait, with a subtle blend of nutrition and attractors, can work season after season. Fact! So I decided I would set out to make my own boilie for the Lagoon campaign. I took quite a ribbing from the boys, because I've been known to be a total shelf-life merchant until now. Not that I chop and change. I've been using The Source from Dynamite for years, and it has worked for me. My view was that in this day and age it's simply not necessary to make your own bait. Dad had always encouraged me to think about how and why something works, but I really couldn't be arsed with all that fiddling about making up six-egg mixes week after week. I've changed my mind though. Those early carp fishing heroes like Rod Hutchinson must have got huge satisfaction from developing their own baits and catching on them. I want a piece of that, and reckon I'll get an edge by using my own ultra-fresh baits on the Lagoon. Maybe it's all in my head, but improving your chances can be down to a few percent here and there – and feeling confident!

In my opinion, the big secret about bait, contrary to what some bait companies would have you believe, is there are no big secrets. Now don't get me wrong, it's not simple or straightforward, and it seems there are many things we don't fully understand, but secrets? I don't think so. I've been trying to get my head round it, and it seems you need a degree in biochemistry to really understand how all the information fits together. Thanks to the Internet though, it's pretty easy to get good quality information and ingredients. It makes you appreciate how much effort the pioneers of High Nutritional Value baits must have put in, the likes of Fred Wilton, Duncan Kay and Geoff Kemp.

I now appreciate that a good quality HNV bait is essentially a one-stop shop for a carp's food requirements. As I understand it that is why you can, given the right baiting strategy, tempt carp to eat them, even in waters which are loaded with naturals. I'm sure you've dragged out weed crawling with water hog louse, shrimps, snails and bloodworm, and thought, "I've got no chance competing with this lot". But it seems carp aren't stupid; they're always on the lookout for a cheap meal, and if you can provide a good one on a regular basis then most carp can be tempted. After all, it may take the carp an hour to eat a kilo of boilies, but several days to get the same nutritional value munching their way through the weed and silt.

So how do you go about making a top quality boilie? Time for a bit of the science I've learnt off the Internet. Believe me if the teachers at school had taught me chemistry through carp diets and bait making I'd have been all ears, rather than falling asleep on my stool at the back of the class. So here goes... the type of nutrients a carp needs can be sorted roughly into two groups, macronutrients and micronutrients. Macronutrients include proteins, fats and carbohydrates. Micronutrients include vitamins, minerals and trace elements. You need to ensure your bait contains all these things in the right quantities.

Proteins are essential for building and maintaining our bodies, our meaty bits if you like. Once they get into the fish's gut they are broken down by enzymes called proteases into smaller molecules called polypeptides, and then further into the building blocks of proteins, amino acids. Apparently there are 22 amino acids required by animals, some of which a carp can synthesise itself, and others, the 'essential' amino acids, which it needs in what it eats. So it makes sense that my boilie has all the essential amino acids in it. And here they are: arginine, histidine, isoleucine, leucine, lysine, methionine, phenylalanine, threonine, tryptophan and valine. No, it doesn't mean much to me either. However, all proteins made for the animal feed industry have a breakdown of the amino acid content, and you can work out the amounts you need to include in your boilie from the carp's requirement per kilo of bait. Still with me? Bloody dull isn't it, but if you want an edge in the bait department I reckon you've got to know this stuff.

You may also have read about the digestibility of proteins. This is another point where I'm a bit hazy, but it seems there are two kinds of protein, fibrous and globular. Globular proteins are easier to break down or digest. And the most widely available and used globular protein is milk protein. This is why people recommend milk protein for winter baits, when the carp's metabolism has slowed right down and is not able to digest food so well. I think we now come to the limits of scientific knowledge, because while we should in theory stick to milk-based globular proteins, studies have shown that fish, and in fact other animals too, grow faster and have better health if they are fed a diet containing fish proteins. I haven't as yet come across a good explanation of why this should be. Instead there are references to *unidentified growth factors*, and the food industry is actively researching what they are. Dad was always saying science doesn't have all the answers; sometimes it just has the questions.

There is a hell of a lot written about proteins, but remember they are only one part of a balanced diet. You also have to think about carbohydrate, fat, minerals and vitamins. And then you come to attractors. There is a school of thought that they are not really necessary, that the bulk ingredients will do the job for you. However, carp anglers being suckers for a good flavour, have long tried all kinds and I'm sure we all have our favourites. Dad used to swear by Bun Spice, and Geoff Kemp's Dairy Cream, whereas I prefer the more pungent meaty and fishy varieties. Other attractors include sweeteners, amino stimulants, essential and bulk oils and appetite stimulators. So where has all this research led me? Up the garden path and into the asylum? Nearly, but I think I have finally arrived at a formula I'm happy to test. It's a nutritionally balanced bait with the added appeal of Monster Crab. *Monster!* Here it is:

6oz fishmeal
2oz soya flour
2oz semolina
2oz robin red
1oz egg albumen
1oz multivitamin supplement
5ml of Monster Crab flavour

A boilie-only approach can put excessive strain on the cash flow, so I've decided to include a couple of particles into my baiting strategy. And if I had to choose one particle to fish with then it would have to be sweetcorn. Everyone knows it's an extraordinary carp catcher, and it's stocked in every food shop in the country. Oh yes, and the plastic stuff catches too. Plastic bait eh? How can carp be so difficult to catch at times, and yet they go around troughing up plastic food? The other killer particle is of course hemp. They love it!

The bait that Ron and Tommy are always talking about in private, are peanuts. You really can't mention them these days, as it's clear that they have been abused in the past. Too many anglers piled bucket loads of them into lakes, week after week, month after month, getting the fish pre-occupied, and literally making the whole stock ill with vitamin deficiencies and associated symptoms. A few waters will allow them in small quantities, but on most lakes they are banned to avoid any potential problems. What it is about peanuts, I'm not sure, but I'm the same as the carp; once I've started eating them I can't get enough. Food for thought, but probably best avoided if you don't want any grief from fellow anglers and fishery owners.

As if to underline that there is nothing new in carp bait, I have just been watching Rob Maylin on *Carp TV* talking about how maggots are so deadly in PVA bags that he has given up fishing nights. He's catching that many during the day, he prefers to go home and sleep in the comfort of his own bed. I'll give the Mag-Aligner a go at some point, but it's on the back burner for now. I've also been reading a lot about mixing up the size and texture of your bait. It makes sense to me; you don't want them getting too settled into feeding in one particular way, the theory being that with different sized and shaped baits they're more likely to make a mistake. What I'm not sure about is how effective it is to blend very small particles like hemp with boilies. I know they love hemp, and I have caught using boilies over a bed of hemp, but that's on hungry waters where almost any tactic will work. The question is; which is the one for the Lagoon? I'm a big fan of sweetcorn, and am in good company. Rod Hutchinson still rates it highly, even after years in the bait business, and Yatesy rarely leaves home without a tin. I think the modern maestro Mr Hearn also uses it on occasions, but is it just too blatant for experienced old fish in the crystal clear Lagoon water? I'll just have to see what happens. I'm 99% decided that the bait for the Lagoon campaign will be my Monster Crab boilies fished over hemp and sweetcorn. *Bring it on!*

Six

And there are carp fishers, or should I say carp addicts.
These are very strange men indeed.

BB, 1950

ur eyes are used to khaki, or red, white and blue of the boating brigade, but rarely do we see a fine suit in the shop. Tommy and I exchange a look, *"Who the hell is this?"*

"I wouldn't park there for long mate, our local Gestapo are pretty trigger-happy with their tickets," I say. The man turns his attention from the rig board.

"Morning, is Tommy around?"

Tommy looks intrigued. "Yes, I'm Tommy, how can I help?"

"Harry Plant," the man says, smiling, holding out a large ring-laden hand and striding confidently across to the counter. "Good to meet you. I'm told you've run this shop for a long time Tommy."

"Yeah, longer than I care to remember."

"I want to talk to you about a new business I'm starting."

"Don't tell me you're opening a tackle shop round here."

"Well, yes I plan too, which is why I wanted to speak to you personally."

"Oh that's bloody marvellous: can you make things any harder up there?" Tommy says, looking up at the ceiling and shaking his fist.

"Don't worry Tommy, it's not competition, I'm here to see if you want to expand," Harry says.

"Expand? I'm barely making ends meet."

"Welcome to the future Tommy, it's called Marsh Lakes!"

"A new fishery, eh?" Tommy says, barely concealing his scepticism. Typical Tommy, constantly looking the other way when something new takes off.

"We moved to Fenstanton last year and built a house on some land out there. I've always wanted my own lakes and so had three dug. The plan is to set up a carp fishery with an on-site tackle shop and café."

"Wow, you kept that quiet! First I've heard of it, and I get to hear most of the local gossip in here," I say.

Harry casts a steely look in my direction. "Good son, and that's how I would like to keep it for now. Tommy, can I have a word in private?"

"You can talk in front of Ron and Kes Harry, they're family. And as you can see we've got tumble weeds rolling around the shop not customers."

Harry stares at Tommy, obviously weighing up the situation.

"Family is good." He smiles and rubs the blond stubble on either side of his mouth with a thumb and forefinger. "Look, I've got an idea that might suit both of us. It's a partnership kind of thing, you and me running a tackle shop at my lakes."

It's Tommy turn to do his Clint Eastwood impression, a couple of gun slingers sizing each other up, working out if the other one is bullshitting

"Partnership? No harm in talking it over I suppose, and I'm definitely interested in seeing these new lakes of yours."

"Alright then, come over on Thursday morning at ten and I'll show you around." He hands Tommy a card, gives Ron and me a nod, then leaves.

"Bloody hell Tommy, you were a bit frosty with him," I say once he's outside.

"In my experience Kes, if it sounds too good to be true, it usually is."

"Fair enough Tommy, but we should at least see whether he's the real deal," Ron says.

"David Dickinson, ITV," I say.

"Can you give it a bloody rest, Kes?!" Tommy says.

"Sorry."

"I'm going over there on Thursday aren't I; we'll take it from there."

It's clear Tommy is not in the mood for our normal banter this morning, so Ron and I wander over to the window. Our new friend is still sitting in his black Range Rover.

"Cool, sports edition, forty six grand's worth!" I say.

"What the...? We've got company!" Ron shouts back towards Tommy.

About twenty people are gathering on the opposite side of the road. It's a ragbag mixture of teenagers, ageing hippies and the odd pensioner thrown in for good measure. At the front is Saira. They're all wearing red T-shirts with *FishAction* printed in bold white letters across the chest.

"It's started then. Rob in Huntingdon Tackle told me he'd had a bit of trouble the other day. Thought they might turn up here sooner or later," Tommy says.

"I'll go out and tell 'em to piss off."

"Nah, leave it Ron. I don't want to aggravate the situation."

"Those banners are really pissing me off, *Stop the cruelty, Ban Fishing*. They're havin' a laugh aren't they?" Ron says.

"Afraid not: they've got the wind in their sails now fox hunting's gone. We're next on the list, ain't that right Kes?"

"Looks like it."

"They're pissing in the wind though, really, aren't they? I mean they reckon there's over a million anglers in the UK," Ron says.

"Let's hope so. I'll call the police, let them sort it out," Tommy says.

Tommy leaves me on watch while he rings the cops. Ron, frustrated at being held on the leash suddenly decides he needs to sort the maggot fridge. My mind drifts off, wondering if maggots are on their list of species to save. They must draw the line somewhere; I mean, surely they don't campaign for bacterial rights. Bemused morning shoppers are giving them a wide berth, crossing over and passing in front of our window. A couple give me the thumbs up, but most keep their heads down keen to get away as fast as possible. There is one positive to the morning's drama, I get to stare at Saira's long legs and curves. Lucky Jay! You've got to admire her, leading the line with her chants and banter. She's a live one all right. I can see they're handing out leaflets, and curiosity gets the better of me.

"Morning Saira; having fun blocking the street and ruining our business?"

"You should be ashamed of yourself, working in that torture shop."

"Yeah, I know, we eat babies too!"

"It's not funny, and you won't be laughing once this campaign gets going. The writing's on the wall for you lot."

"Yeah sure Saira, change the record. Can I have a leaflet? You never know I might see the light."

"Read it, and mend your ways. You're living in the 21st century!"

"Yeah, but my knuckles still scrape along the floor, I'm having trouble standing upright."

She looks at me, and plants a loser sign on her forehead with thumb and forefinger.

"Grow up Kes!"

I give her my best 'I'm really a nice guy' grin, and beat a retreat to the safety of the shop. The front cover of the leaflet shows a dead coot all tangled up in discarded line, an otter hung up on a post, and a keepnet full of fish being dragged out of the water. Maybe it's Saira's physical charms, but I find myself wavering. It's hard to argue in favour of leaving line lying around, and frankly I'm not a fan of keepnets full of fish. Otters though, that's a bit more tricky. I love them and loathe them in equal measure. In many ways they're pretty cool, and undoubtedly awesome anglers themselves. Problem is, they're not really into catch and release, and they can't read. No matter how many signs you put up saying no day tickets, and all fish must be returned, they carry on munching their way through your stock, leaving bits of dead fish all over the place. It's bloody carnage, literally!

"What have you got there Kes, enemy propaganda?" Tommy asks.

"Hot off the press and designed to make an angler's blood boil. Gets you thinking though," I say handing Tommy the leaflet.

"Kes, you always see things in shades of grey, but this is a black and white issue."

"I'm not so sure; we could do a lot to improve our green credentials."

"Green bloody credentials; you don't half talk a load of shite sometimes. We're fen folk, not towny liberals. Hunting, shooting and fishing is a way of life going back hundreds, probably thousands of years," Ron says.

"These kids think meat comes from the supermarket. They've lost the link with nature," Tommy says.

"Alright, relax. I'm just saying most of that lot out there are in Morrissey's camp!"

"You've lost us again Kes: listening to you is like doing the bloody Times cryptic crossword."

"Come on chaps, they're all carrot crunchers, lettuce lovers."

"What they need is a good plate of steak and chips," Ron says. "They're all suffering from iron deficiency. All these pulses and vegetables have turned their brains to mush."

"Maybe you're right, I'll pop down the chippy and get them all saveloy and chips; or maybe a kebab!" I say.

I'm just thinking it's all very tame, when there's a loud thud on the shop window. Someone has lobbed a flour bomb at us. It's a bit sixth form, but Ron bites.

"That's it, I'm gonna have a word!" Out the door he goes, and over the road. "Right then which one of you bastards threw that?"

"None of your business fatty," Saira snarls, and starts another chant.

I have to laugh. Poor old Ron is ready to explode, his fists clenched and face scarlet with rage, but he's totally bamboozled by this blond bombshell waving a banner in his face. He grabs the banner off Saira and snaps the pole on his knee. All he can think to say is, "You want a check up from the neck up darlin'!" Which, when you think about it is pretty poor as put-downs go, and his mood is not improved by me pissing myself laughing as he comes back in the shop.

"Well thanks for all your support lads."

"Sorry Ron, you really told 'em didn't you," I say.

"Don't take the bait Ron," Tommy says.

"Bloody winds me right up!" Ron says still fuming.

"And that's just what they want. I'll let the law sort them out."

"Hang on, here comes the Sweeney!" I say.

A couple of young plods arrive in their Vauxhall Astra, looking excited at the chance of some action. But with flour bombs being the limit of the public disorder on offer today, a few stern words rather than truncheons and handcuffs are all that's required. The whole thing fizzles out by lunchtime. As *FishAction* are preparing to leave, I go outside to thank Saira for stopping by, but only get a scowl. A couple of banners are left propped up against the shop window and the protesters melt away into town. The police give us some guff about patrols day and night, and sleepy old St. Ives nods off again.

"Modern life is Rubbish, eh chaps?" I say.

"Blur, 1993," Tommy says, forcing a smile.

"The country is going down the khazi, that's for sure!" Ron growls.

Seven

Carp can be observed clearing up every piece of bait in the swim except the one with the hook in it. In this case, the solution is the use of the Hair rig... a method of attaching the bait without putting it on the hook at all. This rig was developed by my friend Len Middleton and myself after observing the behaviour of carp in my tank at home.

Kevin Maddocks, 1981

Rig and bait testing takes place at Rivendell fisheries. At least that's my public line on the regular visits I make as it's not cool in certain company to admit you simply enjoy the arm-wrenching action and friendly atmosphere. The whole experience down there is a welcome tonic for those Lagoon blanking blues. Not that it's an out-and-out runs water, or a hole in the ground stuffed with fish; just a nice little mature fenland lake with a fair head of doubles for its three acres and the chance of an occasional 20-pounder. Ron and Tommy are a bit scathing about my trips, saying they'll eat anything, so it's not a good test. Well, maybe, but I feel confident once I've caught a fish on a particular setup and that helps me sit for hour after hour on harder waters. A day off from the shop gave me the chance for a session, so I was lined up with the other punters at 7.30 this morning, waiting for the electronic gates to open at 8 o'clock sharp. The forecast for the day was flood and tempest, not what you expect in June, so I wimped out and chose one of the car park swims where I can simply back the Passat in and fish out of the boot. Camper tactics I know, but why get soaked when the fish are cruising a rod length out?

I've got a few Lagoon rig ideas to test out, and the new Monster Crab boilies. While I was sitting in the car this morning waiting for the gates to open I got thinking about the history of rigs and how things have changed over the years. I reckon the two biggest developments in carp-fishing history have been the invention of the Hair rig and the Korda Underwater series. Now, I'm sure you'll have other ideas, but hear me out. You see, having recently read Izaak's bible, it seems that until 1981 when Middleton and

Maddocks unveiled the mind-blowing Hair rig to the world, not much had changed since the *Compleat Angler* was published over 300 years earlier. Blimey, that can't be right surely? Well, no of course it's not strictly true; there were lots developments in between. As I found out from Ron, this geezer Otto Overbeck was doing some pretty advanced things way back in the early 1900s, and then of course, you can't ignore the contributions of people like Richard Walker in the '50s and '60s, and succeeding generations, who began to develop specialist carp tackle, watercraft and boiled baits: the cult of carp fishing we know and love today. These things were important, I admit, but carp fishing was still exclusive and frankly difficult for the average angler. The belief that life is too short for carp fishing was still widely held. This all changed with the development and publication of the Hair rig. All hail the late great, Lenny Middleton and his more famous pal Kevin Maddocks. Their pioneering work in Kevin's test tank was a true revolution. It was like discovering fire or inventing the wheel; life was transformed. Suddenly, a massive piece of the carp fishing jigsaw was handed out to everyone.

Carp Fever was published ten years before I was born. It was an old book by the time I was on the banks, but I read it over and over, devouring the little gems it contains, absorbing the names and places, the stories of historic captures and carp. Dad loved it; he thought Maddocks was a carp fishing god. I think he admired the attention to detail, the total commitment, organisation and sheer tenacity of the man, probably appealed to his military mind, and let's face it we're all guilty of being little boy-soldiers, talking about campaigns and battles, dressed from head to toe in camo clothing. But the Hair rig, that was undoubtedly genius, and together they were responsible for the single most important development in carp fishing ever, period, full stop, end of story. No not the end of this story, but think about it; pretty much every bait attachment development since has been some kind of adaptation of the basic Hair rig idea.

Just the cover was magic, on the front, Kevin with 'She' from the School Pool, Faversham, and Sir Peter on the back with his brace of upper-thirty Yeoveney mirrors. All hail Sir Pete! *Monster!* Like dad, I was totally dazzled by KM's commitment, the record keeping, the analysis of weather and results, particularly his debunking of winter-carping myths. Some of it is fantastically obsessive. Check this out:

"My bedchair is normally placed so that the side of the front leg is no more than one inch from the left-hand rear rod rest... I position my boots standing up beside the left-hand side of the bedchair and never zip up the sleeping bag further than waist level, and in fact, I purposely damaged the zips so they cannot travel any further than this... I have always disciplined myself not to get too comfortable at night as this can also lead to inefficiency."

Brilliant, love it, and accompanied by a series of photos demonstrating how he strikes from his half-zipped bag and dons his strategically placed boots. I suppose this setup was designed before the Hair rig, when you had to really time your strike and set home the hook. You should see me getting out of my bag at night. People run the marathon quicker than me getting to my rods. The man was light years ahead of most of his fellow '70s carp anglers. Just check out his three-rod setup with his signature KM carbon rods and Abu Cardinal reels.

Like the Hair rig, the Korda Underwater DVDs blew my mind. It was like I had been fishing blind for years. And then the lord that is Danny – all hail Danny – said let there be light and there was light, and cameras and action, and lots of scenes with Danny running backwards and forwards from the camera bivvy, getting excited, frustrated, out of breath and trying desperately not to swear. Awesome! I watched them over and over, pondering the dynamics of that critical moment when the carp sucks and blows your bait. What a puzzle! Finding the balance between getting your bait taken and maximum hooking efficiency completely does my head in and keeps me awake at night. It was amazing to see the monster carp at Wellington Country Park in part five picking up and ejecting the rigs so easily. And that was in situations when the fish were really having it. I'm only going to have a fraction of the chances. Makes you wonder how we ever nail a fish.

I've been racking my brains and trawling through hundreds of articles trying to decide on the rig for the Lady. Terry Hearn seems to restrict himself to a few specific rigs for particular situations, the popped-up Hinged Stiff rig and now the Choddy being firm favourites. The beauty of the Choddy is that you can present a bait over weed and silt, and cast with confidence at showing fish. Having this in your armoury will give you a definite edge, but I need to build my confidence in it, because it really does look too blatant. I've also heard that if you don't set it up exactly right you're prone to dropping fish, not something mere mortals could stand when fishing the Lagoon. I've been told the curve is the thing to get right and I think Terry Hearn recommends not using a hook smaller than a size five. You really want an aggressive setup, to *grab them and not let go*. I'm playing around with different ways of masking the hook without reducing its hooking properties. One idea is to glue a niblet of plastic corn or a fake maggot on the shank, but it's a bedchair idea and needs fieldtesting. Rod one will be fished Choddy style, or maybe the Hinged Stiff rig, depending on which swim I'm in.

On the second rod I'm going for a Snowman rig, size six Korda Wide Gape, 20cm of Sufix Black Silt coated braid, and a 2½oz clipped Fox lead. My edge on this rig will be to strip back a hinge on the Combi-Link about 4cm from the hook, but leave those final 4cms coated. I then stick on a blob of rig putty just behind the hinge. This gives it some flexibility on the way in, but also retains stiffness and angle by the hook, which in my befuddled mind makes it less likely to flip over if blown and, in theory, less likely to come back out. It also gives it a 360° effect, as whichever angle the fish sucks from, the rig swivels round on the hinge with the hook going in the mouth facing forward. The rig putty should also pull the hook point down onto the bottom lip. Cunning or what? I recently read that Kevin Nash feels many anglers miss out on an edge by using short Hairs, and that it actually reduces the efficiency of many rigs. I can see what he's getting at; after all, the whole idea of the Hair is to separate the hook from the bait. Yeah, long Hairs rule!

I'm hedging my bets on the third rod and sticking with a straight mono hooklink, and this one is so simple, so effective, low visibility with great anti-eject and anti-tangle qualities. I have confidence in this rig – well, providing the fish approach it from the front or side. Hang on, that's right, I remember now: I do worry that if the fish troughs up along the main line, the stiffness of the mono will prevent the hook going in. Could maybe tie in a ring swivel 3cm from the hook?. This would give it more movement, but too many knots for my liking. Oh bugger, watch this space, it could all change again depending on which way the wind is blowing and which article I've just read!

The three different rigs are out in the Rivendell margins with pop-up and bottom versions of the new boilie recipe. A couple of hours pass, and I'm sitting on my unhooking mat in the boot staring through the rain drops at my muddy pitch, trying to remember why I thought this would boost my confidence. Frustration. And what the hell is going on with the weather, it's supposed to be flaming June? This was supposed to be a walk in the park, light relief, a bit of practice for the real thing, but it's in danger of turning into yet another blank. Maybe Tommy was right. He said my rigs would be too crude, that I should scale right down for these pressured doubles. I'm certainly not learning much, sitting here blanking my arse off. I can do that on the Lagoon. The odd fish crashes here and there, but no obvious pattern. I slump back in the chair and reach into my bag for a bit of comfort food. What do I have to do to get a take? Halfway into the second Bounty bar, while nibbling off the chocolate from the coconut with my front teeth, line tightens on the left-hand rod, the spool spins and string streaks through the rings. Fish on! The Snowman Combi rig has done the business!

My body knows exactly what to do and in what order. Springing from the back of the car, Bounty bar is thrust fully into gob, left hand grabs rod and lifts, while right simultaneously turns the handle to engage clutch. Rod compresses into battle curve and line clicks from spool as fish makes dash for reeds. Adrenalin pumping, I yell out loud, a mixture of relief, sheer joy and shock at being connected with raw power after several hours of stillness, reflection and doubt. The fish keeps deep in the water and is surprisingly determined. It feels heavy as it bores away, but being tackled up for the Lady, I let it know who's in charge. A few minutes later it rolls on the surface ten yards to my left against the reed line, head lolling over. A couple of further lunges and it's soon in the net, a nice mid-double common, the Korda Wide Gape lodged nicely in the middle of the bottom lip. Job done, rig works, bait works, no need for a number or photo, just lower the net cord, and the fish swims strongly out of sight. Suddenly all is well; I'm the man again!

That fish came from the margin, and so I decide to put all three rods back in the edge, one on a Hinged Stiff rig and two on Choddies. For some reason they weren't having it this morning, but once they get onto your bait in here you can usually winkle out another. They're pretty cute though, and seem to know what time they're at risk. If you haven't had a bite in the first hour, things are generally a bit slow until, strangely, the middle of the day and then again between six and seven before the fishery closes for the night. They probably all line up by the car park at seven watching the cars leave one by one, giving each other the all clear: "Come on boys and girls time to really get stuck into all the tucker those silly buggers have spodded into the lake all day long."

I really need a bite on a Choddy. To be honest it doesn't really look like the one, but everyone tells me they work a treat. I haven't quite worked out the best bite indication for this rig, but I am going with Jim Shelley's advice of having the line nice and slack and bobbins hanging straight down from the buzzer. I figure that fishing the margin there's only one way they can go, away from me. Ten minutes later, I'm in again, and it's the Choddy on the middle rod. I watched the line tighten up and hit it before the bobbin moved or bite alarm sounded. Now I'm curious to see what the hook hold is like and whether I actually get the little terrier in the net. It's charging about all over the place, giving a mighty account of itself. Looks to be one of the better fish, a nice fully-scaled mirror of around 20lb. She glides over the net cord without much fuss, and my first fish on a Chod rig is secured. Interestingly when I go to remove the hook, it's lying in the net mesh. Question; are Choddies prone to hookpulls?

I sit there for another five hours, expectation of a run growing the closer it gets to chucking out time. Fish start showing all over the place, and the temptation is to put baits on their heads. Several of the lads are adopting this tactic, but I notice no one has had a bite since my last fish. I decide to sit on my hands, and wait for one to munch its way along the marginal reeds. I'm still fully expecting a take right up until the limit, ten past seven. If I don't reel in now I'll be risking a ban by having to ask the owner to open the gates for me. Wouldn't be the first time. I bring the first rod in and pack it into the holdall. Just as I'm about to remove the middle rod it rips off: I pull into it, but there's nothing there. Looking down I see a big boil in the water. Whether it was a liner or I was done over is annoyingly difficult to say. Oh well, that's my lot for the day. At least I know carp will eat the new Monster Crab baits. One of my rigs definitely works, but still a few doubts hanging over the Choddies.

Eight

*A true record of the life of an habitual carp fisher would be a book
to set beside De Quincy's Confessions of an Opium Eater. A book
of taut nerves, of hallucinations, of a hypnotic state, of visions,
Japanese in character of great blunt headed, golden fish in sprays of
weeping willow, and then rare moments when this long drawn-out
tautness of expectation is resolved into a frenzy of action.*

Arthur Ransome, 1929

I'm down the Lagoon for a quick overnighter, full of confidence in the new bait after the session down at Rivendell. However, things are a bit slower over here, so I thought I'd show you round my swim, what gear I've managed to get my hands on and, most importantly, a look at my special bivvy. I mentioned I'm the proud owner of a Titan bivvy, but it's not exactly standard issue. One morning shortly after its purchase I was lying staring up at the pristine fabric, breathing strange new synthetic smells, and had a strong urge to make it mine, customize Mr Nash's original design. Of course there's nothing wrong with a standard olive green finish, but it's just not in my nature to be in the herd. Growing up, we lived in a row of identical council houses, and I was always trying to get dad to spray it bright orange or lime green. Dad wouldn't have it, of course, he said he was already going out on a limb having his family outside the barracks, and he could do without upsetting the neighbours and the council with a wacky paint job. I think any self-respecting bivvy tramp should make his mark on his bankside home, don't you? Imagine 'Pimp my Ride' and you'll get the picture. I got the inspiration for my design from our drummer, who has an awesome gothic drum wrap, all skulls, serpents and semi-naked sirens.

So let me give you a guided tour. It won't take long, there's basically inside, and outside. As you approach from afar, the first thing you'll notice, particularly if it's dark, is a glowing white image painted on the rear panel. It's Jim Root's Slipknot mask in luminescent paint. WICKED! *Radiation's* lead singer Jethro did it for me. Jethro's not his real name, you can't be a death metal singer called Kevin. Sorry, I'm slipping off the point. If it's really late and I've already crashed, the door will be down and you'll see Jethro's second contribution, a skull and cross bones, intended to strike fear and anxiety into unwary trespassers. You should never creep up on a bivvy tramp. They are basically friendly individuals, but ferociously territorial. You have been warned! As dawn breaks a very classy, self-styled camo paint job appears. None of your meticulous Realtree realism for a bivvy tramp, my camouflage owes more to the Jackson Pollock school of painting, just bloody spray it on with some passion. I'm not sure Kevin, that's Mr Nash not Jethro, would approve, but then again it could catch on. Watch out for a gothic design in their next catalogue.

That's basically all there is to say about the outside, now come in and check out my funky interior. Firstly, what do you think of this, my black fake fur bed cover? Luxury! You'll have to get one before everyone else does. They're the dogs! Looking back out across the Lagoon, my adoption of modern psychology hits you. On the inside of the window panels I've attached a couple of laminated A4 pictures, on the left is the Lady and on the right the Black Pig. While I lie there gazing out at stationary bobbins, I'm visualising success. You may think it's obsessive and pointless, but I say it's motivational, and gives me a mental edge. Or am I just mental? Don't ask Ron and Tommy about that, they're so unimaginative and out of touch with modern sports psychology. I may be going over the top with this, but everything I read on Wikipedia tells me success is a state of mind.

On the floor by the door is my newest purchase. It's called a Safari chef and has, without wishing to overstate the case, transformed my life. No longer do I have to suffer balancing crappy old aluminium pans with dodgy folding handles on my little Coleman stove. Don't get me wrong, the Coleman's fine; driven by unleaded rocket fuel, it's guaranteed to warm the bivvy and your Bombay Bad Boy Pot Noodles on the coldest of winter nights. But this new piece of kit comes with a wok-style pan, a grill rack, a frying pan and a barbecue griddle, all for fifty notes off *ebay*. Nice! A Lagoon bivvy tramp has to eat well: you can't fish on an empty stomach. Ron and Tommy can't believe their luck. Suddenly from being the biggest scrounger on the complex who'd live for 48 hours on a packet of biscuits, three Pot Noodles, and a bag of Haribos, I'm suddenly whipping up all kinds of pukka tucker for the three of us. I can't get enough of Aunty Nigella on the iPlayer, the saucy cow! You can keep Jamie and Gordon, I like a bit of posh, puts me right in the mood for a feast. I've already planned the menu for our next session, a good old fry up for breakfast – tasty – followed by tomato and chilli pasta for lunch, and chicken curry for dinner, washed down with bottles of Bishops Finger.

On the other side of the door I keep my prize possession, an original canvas ARVN rucksack, made in America and issued to soldiers in the Army of the Republic of Vietnam back in the early '70s. Dad gave it to me for my birthday a couple of years ago. It's perfect for short sessions, lots of pockets, and built to last; no crappy zips or straps that are going to break. I did have a bit of a disaster last year, I left it out one night with some boilies in the front pocket, and the bastard rats gnawed their way into it. Had to get mum to do a repair job. Anyway I think that's just about covered the bivvy, let's go outside and have a look at the business end of my new premier-league carp kit.

Now I have to confess, I persuaded mum to lend me a grand, and have gone a bit over the initial budget. I've pretty much wiped out my savings and stacked up a debt, but check these rods and reels out, they're to die for. I had my heart set on some Daiwa SS3000s but they're just impossible to get for less than about £200 each, even second hand. I started looking at other Daiwa reels and Ron put me onto the Daiwa Infinity-X 5000s. They're big, but the spools are great for casting, the line lay is good, and the clutch is awesome. They've also got a Baitrunner-style feature, which I personally like. I wanted four, but found someone flogging a set of three on *ebay*, and managed to get them for £430. I'll save up and buy a spare one at some point. The question then was what would be a good match for such beasts. I looked at going for a set of 3lb test curve Infinity rods, but couldn't find any for less than £230 each. So check these babies out, ESP MK2 Terry Hearn's, 12' 9", 3.25lbers with full Fuji SIC guides and full Duplon handle. Nice! Got them for £130 each: result!

Not much else to report. Got the JRC unhooking cot thingy, otherwise everything is pretty much as it was. Next on the wish list is a set of these new Nash buzzers. Bloody hell hi-tech or what? I read somewhere, that there's more computing power in those kiddies than was used to get Neil Armstrong on the moon. Got to have some of that! Talking of hi-tech reminds me, I used some of mum's money to get an iPhone. Oh my God, I'm in cyber-geek heaven! What you can't do with this bit of kit is hardly worth doing. I can check out *ebay* from my bedchair, watch Nigella on the iPlayer (I like an older woman), listen to the football, and, most importantly, get onto Metcheck for the latest weather forecasts.

Totally knackered; time to get in the sack. For a while I watch the sun going down over the trees, a few clouds reflecting the last of the light, the whole sky slowly turning pink, then grey and finally black. Drifting off; the day slipping away. Next thing I know I'm wide awake again, and it's still completely dark. I pull out my iPhone, three o'clock in the morning, feeling wired, mind racing. Try to unwind and focus on my breathing, keep my mind still, relax my body. No good. It's bloody impossible this meditation lark, I've got so much to think about! No not Boilies, everyone's using them. It's weedy, so I want something smelly, and I want them to root about for it. Luncheon meat keeps popping into my head. Don't be a plonker Kes, you work in a tackle shop full of modern baits. Plus Tommy and Ron will have a field day with that idea. But I'm only fishing in the margins and it's different. No, it's just too retro: Monster Crab boilies on two rods and a particle on the other, probably plastic corn. Come on Kes, one hookbait not three. Maybe the boilies tipped with plastic corn? Aaahh yes, now we're talking!

This is getting out of hand. Right, England back four: John Terry, Phil Jagielka, Ashley Cole, Glen Johnson. What about Rio Ferdinand? Rigs. Mono, fluoro or braid? Long, yes long, 18 inches, everyone is fishing short. Hinged Stiff rig, size fives, short Hair. How do you pop up luncheon meat? Forget luncheon meat. Running or fixed leads. I just don't like fixed leads. Slack lines and no bobbins. Midfield. Gerrard, Barry, Lampard, Johnson. You can't play Gerrard and Lampard in the same team can you?

One tin of meat and half a kilo of tigers every other night. Forget the bloody meat. Just after dark, don't want to be seen. Rooney definitely, but is Defoe fit enough? What about Bent? Can't start without Crouch! Will have to be short sessions, too busy in the shop. Naked ladies. At last a real diversion, Scarlett Johansson, Katy Perry, naked in my bivvy. Need to stock up on PVA bags. No, that's it, really can't sleep, not now. Will have to go for a walk up the track.

Call the doctor, I'm not well: it's another bad case of carp fever!

Nine

*After a time, you may find that 'having' is not so
pleasing a thing, after all, as 'wanting'.*

Dr Spock, USS Enterprise, stardate 3372.7

ommy and I pull up outside Harry's gate. Through the fence we can see the
lakes nestling at the bottom of a short grassy slope, right on the edge of the
Ouse flood plain. Pressing the intercom elicits a chirpy voice: "Morning chaps,
come in."

We drive along the gravel track to a parking area. Harry's impressive mansion is to our
left, and we suddenly regret our jeans and jumper approach.

"God bless our standard of living," I say.

"Paul Simon, 1975," Tommy says.

Harry emerges through the large ornate front door, again sporting his blue pin-striped
business suit, pink shirt and gold cufflinks. The only concession to the country setting is a
pair of very clean green Hunter wellies.

"Welcome Chaps. Let's go and have a look at the lakes. I'll show you what I'm
planning."

"Lovely house, Harry!" I say.

"We like it Kes."

"I can see you take security seriously."

"I'm spending serious money on fish, Tommy, I don't want some scum-bag knocking
them off in the small hours. These razor wire fences and CCTV are my insurance
premium. I'm looking for a bailiff and site manager, someone who can look after himself
and deal with any trouble."

"I think we know someone who may fit the bill!"

"Good Tommy, we'll talk about that later. Here it is then, my Monsters Lake. Four
acres of fishing heaven."

"When you say monsters, what do you have in mind?" I ask.

"Well I'm planning about thirty fish for it. Ten 30s, ten 40s, five 50s and five the size of which England has never seen before."

"Bloody hell, I see what you mean. Fish that size don't come cheap," Tommy says.

"This lake is called Willow. It's about five acres and will have five 40s, fifty 30s, and a hundred 20s. The third lake is the three-acre runs lake over there, which will be stuffed full of doubles. I'm going to try an American system on that lake, called prize fishing. We'll put electronic tags on a certain number of fish, with prizes from £10 to £100 if you catch one."

"Very impressive; blows away every other fishery I know! Anglers will flock to it from all over the country," Tommy says.

"Oh yeah, it's special all right. It's taken a lot of planning and dosh to get that many lumps."

"Where are they coming from?" I ask.

"Oh, here and there," Harry says vaguely, "you don't need to worry about that."

"That prize fishing idea sounds like a money spinner," Tommy says, changing the subject.

"Sounds like fun don't it?" Harry says. "Gotta have a laugh, it's only fishing after all."

"What did you have in mind as far as the tackle shop is concerned?" Tommy asks.

"Let's talk business."

Harry leads us over to a pale green table and chairs on the lawn. He looks every inch the nouveau country squire, framed by his house and lakes.

"I like anglers, my sort of people. I'm happy to have them on my lakes. But I also like the best, and if they want the best they have to pay for it. Fishing at Marsh Lakes won't be cheap."

"Sounds reasonable. I think people will pay good money for the kind of fishing you're talking about."

"I'm glad you think so, Tommy. I want this place to make money. I like making money and I like fishing. We're sitting on my bank, and I'll have a bivvy permanently set up here. I think of the bivvy as the new shed. But my shed will have satellite TV for the footy and a barbecue for steak sarnies."

"I like it Harry. Home from home," Tommy says.

It's clear Harry's not a regular bivvy tramp, more of a bivvy baron. You've got to admire him: he wanted lakes, he's got them; he wanted lumps, they're coming. He should have gone the whole hog and built his home closer to the lake, so he could fish from his lounge!

"I like camping up to a point lads, but you need a few luxuries, and entertainment when the fish aren't havin' it. After all fishing is a leisure activity, and modern carping, to me, is all about indulgence. Don't get me wrong, you have to admire the Terry Hearns, and Nigel Sharps but most of us simply don't have the time to do it their way. I also need to take care of business, so we'll have wi-fi for laptops across the site."

"So will the tackle shop sell tickets and bait?" Tommy asks.

"Yes, plus end tackle. They'll only be allowed to use Marsh Lakes' bait and rigs, bought on site. And we'll provide landing nets and unhooking mats in every swim."

"Different Harry," I say.

"Different for a reason. I don't want my fish swimming around with dangerous, badly tied, under-strength rigs hanging out of their gobs. I don't want people bringing disease onto the lakes in their mangy nets, and I don't want them poisoning my fish with their crap baits."

"All very reasonable Harry. And you're looking for someone to run the tackle shop?"

"Yes Tommy, but I also want a café. I don't want anglers messing up the place with their tins, tea bags and turds. Definitely no shitting in the bushes at Marsh Lakes! I'll build the shop and café over there," Harry says pointing to a plot of land on the southern perimeter overlooking Monsters. "I think you'll like it when you see the plans. What do you reckon, are you interested?"

"I am Harry. I really didn't think I would be, but I am. I can see you're a man who gets things done. But why me?"

"Why not? Put it there partner," Harry says, holding out his large gold-adorned hand. Tommy looks a bit shocked at the sudden conclusion to their business meeting.

"I'm a bit anxious Harry," he says putting out his own hand tentatively, "it's all happened so fast."

"Why hang around? We've got work to do."

Tommy doesn't look convinced. "Presumably you'll put a contract together."

Harry waves his hand vaguely, "Yeah, of course, no problem."

"OK, that's good. I'm pretty much running on empty over in St. Ives, with not much spare cash floating around to start up another business."

"Don't worry about that, I'll see you do alright out of it. I'm not interested in running the shop myself, too busy with other things: I just want someone I can trust. We'll work out a fair split."

Harry takes us over to the spot where the shop will be and describes what he has in mind. It does sound good; certainly a hell of a lot bigger and more modern than Tommy's Tackle. We are really struggling, what with Huntingdon Tackle and the Internet. Harry is striding round, pacing out the shop footprint, chatting with Tommy about the details of what we'll stock and how much we'll charge for different things. Poor old Tommy looks a bit bewildered by this human dynamo who has just press-ganged him. It's all a bit tame for my taste though. After all, it's basically fishing in Harry's back garden.

"What do you reckon then, Kes?" Tommy asks, both of them suddenly focused on my response.

"Oh well, I think it's err…, you know, incredible really. Right here in Fenstanton."

"Incredible eh; is that good or a bad?" Harry asks.

"A great business, people will love it!"

"Not you though!"

"Oh don't worry about him Harry, he's obsessed with catching the Lady from the Lagoon. Can hardly think or talk about anything else."

"We'll see how he feels after he's seen some of the proper carp I'm stocking."

Proper carp? Wrong 'uns more like. I change the subject.

"Do you work round here Harry?"

"Full of questions ain't he?"

"Oh that's our Kes, always thinking aren't you mate?"

Seems like I've started on the off beat with Harry, but he's difficult to read, and the way he stares at you is scary; lights on but nobody home. He looks respectable enough, smart suits, pink shirts, but the bling, the tattoos poking out around his neck line, and the eyes, the bloodshot staring eyes, give a different and worrying message. After an uncomfortable pause Harry responds.

"Rubbish!"

"Sorry, I didn't mean to be rude," I say.

"No, you plonker, rubbish, you know, recycling. I've got a waste recycling plant up on the A10 near Wisbech."

"Oh cool, yeah I suppose there's a lot of it about," I say, trying to sound interested.

"Priceless, ain't he Tommy? Anyway come up to the house, we'll have a beer to celebrate."

Harry's house is about 50 metres up a sweeping lawn. It's huge, rendered with a cream painted finish. Large green French windows give views out on to Monsters Lake and the Ouse marshes beyond. Inside, the kitchen is cavernous with grey granite worktops everywhere and a cooker so big you could feed the army with it. Harry takes off his boots, and indicates that we should do the same. Of course there's a flipping great hole in the toe of my right sock, which makes me feel even more out of place in such luxury. Embarrassment about my sock situation is increased by the sudden appearance of a tall blond woman wearing a short silk wrap.

"Ooooh, sorry boys, didn't realise we had company," she says smiling and pulling her skimpy wrap together with her right hand, but leaving her long tanned legs on display.

"Ah Georgia, meet my new friends Tommy and Kes," Harry says.

"Pleased to meet you," she says, coming over and shaking hands, giving me a very stimulating view of her chest. "Lovely long hair Kes!"

"Thanks Mrs P, you too!" I say.

"Looks like a bloody girl," Harry says, smiling, "and what the hell is that you're wearing?"

"Slipknot," I say, pulling my Fox ripstop jacket apart to reveal a particularly gruesome t-shirt.

"Kes is our local head banger," says Tommy.

"Don't you listen to him, he's just jealous cos he's going bald and the last record he bought was Bucks Fizz."

"Shut up you silly tart!" Harry says, squeezing her bum as he walks past.

"Right then, how about I show you my fishing room."

"Oh Harry they don't want to see your silly old fishing rods."

"Course they do darlin', they're as potty about carp as I am."

Harry leads the way out of the kitchen.

Tommy whispers, "You can put your tongue back in now Kes, you're dribbling down your T-shirt."

"Wouldn't say no," I say.

"What's that?" Harry asks.

"Just saying what an amazing setup you've got here," Tommy says.

"Wait till you see this!"

Harry opens the door on to a room stuffed full of tackle. The whole of the far wall is covered with rods on a custom-made rack. To the right is a rig board, bigger than the one we have at Tommy's Tackle, and on the left is a row of four freezers. The middle of the room has a small table with a lamp and a chair surrounded by various tackle bags and boxes.

"Blimey, you didn't tell us you had your own tackle shop already Harry," I say.

"Something I've always wanted, my own little fishing room. Fed up with being stuck out in the garage."

"Very nice. Look at these rods," Tommy says inspecting the rack.

I join him and we marvel at the line of mouth-watering wands.

"This lot must be worth a fortune," I say. "Free Spirits, Harrisons, Greys. And the reels, it's like a Daiwa and Shimano showroom."

Harry is laughing, "Yeah I know, I'm a right tackle tart ain't I?"

"You must have been fishing for a long time Harry, to get all this gear together, and all the vintage carp stuff too," I say pawing an ABU Cardinal 55 like it was some holy relic.

"Oh no, I only started five years ago. Most of it's bought off ebay, can't stop buying the bloody stuff. My PayPal account has taken a right bashing."

"See Tommy, Harry's got a PayPal account. Tommy would rather keep his money under the bed."

"Well it's not a bad idea, bankers are a bunch of crooks," Harry says, "but you've got to move with the times."

"Are you listening Tommy?" I say.

"We'll see; might not need to sell on the net now."

"Oh you've got to get on the web Tommy, it's the future."

"Thank you Harry," I say.

Tommy changes the subject. "You got the fever bad didn't you?"

"Like you wouldn't believe. Georgia thought I'd totally lost the plot, but she's just about come to terms with it now."

"At least she won't be a carp widow from now on," Tommy says, "she can either find you in here or in the garden!"

We all laugh and continue marvelling at Harry's carp fishing collection.

Successful anglers are all naturalists at heart. They try hard to understand how carp behave and respond to changes in their environment.

Jim Gibbinson, Carp Sense, 1992

ack from Harry's and in the library reading a cracking little book, *The Biology of Freshwater Fish,* looking for information on fish senses and natural carp diets. If I want to mix it with the big boys I need to find a few edges, and figure the appliance of a bit of science might help. I'm amazed to discover that fish don't actually exist! Get this, apparently some fish, such as lung fish are more closely related to four legged animals than other fish, and this book says it's not possible to make a list of features, scales, fins, etc. that the animals we all think of as fish have in common. So the fish boffins have decided there isn't a group of animals called fish!

Anyway, apart from this bizarre revelation, the book has a lot of useful information. Did you know that carp are great at smelling, having around 270 million olfactory cells? This makes them about twice as good at smelling as salmon and trout, and an amazing two million times better than humans. I think that could be an edge for wary carp. Surely if a bait smells strong to us, then it must blow a carp's head off? Food for thought! They are not the best sniffers in our waters though, as both eels and catfish are reckoned to be better! I've also found a terrific American study about the contents of carp intestines. They contained 20% green plant material, 30% detritus from the bottom and a whole variety of insect larvae. In one river, over 200 carp were investigated and found to contain an average of 43% crayfish in their guts. No wonder those French carp grow big; hot weather and crayfish for breakfast, lunch and supper.

Encouraged by my new-found knowledge, I whip out the laptop and give *Google* a hammering trying to find a few more edges courtesy of our egghead icthyologist friends. I find a cool e-zine site that has articles summarising carp related research papers. This one looks interesting, *Tracking Winter Carp.* Researchers have tracked carp in ice-covered lakes, and found that they move from deep to shallow areas in search of better oxygenated water. Not much use to me though, I won't be fishing if the Lagoon is frozen over. Another interesting one about *Terminator Fish* catches my eye. It starts:

We love carp, but Australians can't stand them, and have bred a 'terminator fish' which could wipe out the carp down-under. Carp were introduced into Australia more than 100 years ago, and have so much sex in the warm weather they are practically climbing the banks. A new technique in genetic modification has been developed which prevents fish from developing female embryos. These 'Terminator Carp' will breed with other carp spreading the modified gene, resulting in fewer and fewer females. The result? Some scientists say, eventually a male-only population, and the end of carp down-under!

Well they can keep their bloody terminator fish; we like our big girls over here in England. The best article is... *Musical bait?*

Scientists in the U.S. have found that carp are able to learn the difference between blues legend John Lee Hooker and classical composer Bach. In experiments, the carp literally rammed the speaker playing the piece of music that led to a food pellet reward. Many animals have been taught to associate sound with food, starting with the classic Pavlov's dog experiment, where dogs could be made to drool to the sound of a bell. But this is the first time a fish has been shown to have similar skills. So, rather than adding extra flavour to your baits, could a musical rig improve your catches?

That would be hilarious wouldn't it? If instead of Peaches and Cream and Tutti Frutti, you had the choice of The Kooks or Lilly Allen. What would the Lady like? I think she'd go for a bit of Queen, *Fat bottomed girls*. The Black Mirror would have been a sucker for something a bit more hard core, some Pantera maybe, or Marilyn Manson. Your baiting strategy might involve casting out an underwater speaker linked by a wireless signal to your . They'd find all your lovely boilies and scoff away to their favourite tunes. Then, when you're ready to fish, you don't need lots of bait out there, just play them the music and the feeding frenzy begins. I wonder!

Eleven

*I had spent most weekends and three to four nights a week on the lake
and in all that time had only seen about six fish.*

Peter Springate, on his 1978 Yeoveney campaign.

Top five ways to start the day:

Wrapped around the new brunette

A coffee in the bedchair with a warm southerly blowing

Casting at rolling carp

St. Ives soul-food breakfast at the Café

Under the duvet watching Sunday's Match of the Day

nfortunately, currently being without a new brunette, or even an old one, number one on the list is out, but I am enjoying a number two. A nuclear strength brew is working its magic, taking the edge off those Lagoon blankin' blues. Artificial stimulants and carp, nice! Through the bivvy door I can see my silent rods down on the beach aimed at the big Island. I console myself, again, that Terry H took 50 nights to get a bite, and recount the mantra, *one bite is all I need*. Not necessarily true but very therapeutic. I am in the foothills of my Lagoon ascent; oxygen mask, crampons, and Kendall mint cake are still tucked in the rucksack.

"Hey Ho Kes, coming up the Café for brekkie. We can chat about Marsh Lakes?"

"Not today Ron. I'm close, I can smell success in the air."

"I can smell your disgusting coffee, not sure about success!"

"Stimulates the mind and body, Ron. Surely what a man gets up to in the comfort of his own bivvy is his business?"

"You can do what you like as far as I'm concerned. Want me to get you a bacon roll?"

"Ron, you're a brother of the angle and a gentleman!"

"Now you're taking the piss, and that will be £2.50 please!"

"Very good, yes, I see where you're coming from, existential analysis of the situation" I say giggling.

"This isn't Saturday morning philosophy club. What else have you got in that coffee?"

"Great idea," I bellow as Ron marches towards town, "we can start when you get back!"

Still highly amused and amazed in equal measure by, well, everything really, I settle back in my day chair. Coffee in hand, head in the clouds, watching waves rolling into the beach, I feel totally, you know, in tune, in the zone. My reward is a bar of gold rising from the grey and silver reflections off the western edge of the island. *Exceptional!* A beautiful Lagoon common leaping in my swim. Me, the recently promoted camper, entertaining scaly guests in my swim. Excellent!

And with that it's away. The stillness shattered by urgent activity along my string and a banshee wail from the right-hand EOS. Away from the rod physical reactions are somewhat slowed. Coffee is returned to the Earth, as is the custom at this point in the ritual, and co-ordination summoned from deep memory. I finally arrive on the beach, and haul the rod up and back. But the haul goes on, right over my head and backwards, falling, sitting, staring. What the ****? Nothing! Stillness! I stare blankly at a bow wave disappearing round the corner of the island. It's all over! I'm still sitting on the beach beside my rod when Ron returns.

"What are you up to now?"

I lie back and gaze up at the bleak grey clouds.

"Don't tell me you've just lost a fish!" Rons barks.

Both hands cover my face, and a small moan is all I can manage in reply.

"What a mare! Come on, what happened? I'll bloody brain you if it was a dodgy knot."

"Not sure. Haven't wound in yet," I groan.

"It was probably a bream or a tench," Ron says.

I shake my head. "No, I saw it steam off by the island, like a bloody speedboat."

"Hookpull then?"

"Yeah, I reckon, the line was pouring out but when I picked up the rod there was absolutely nothing there. What the hell is that all about?"

"I told you to go longer. It probably just nicked the fish on the edge of the mouth, and when you pulled into it the hook slipped away."

I stand up and wind in slowly. I'm relieved that the rig seems to be in tact.

"Look at this," I say holding up the hooklink.

"What did I tell you?"

Right on the end of my size 6 is a single scale from a large Lagoon common.

C'est la Guerre!

I could have fished the rest of the day, but after the gut-wrenching disaster of this morning, sitting there brooding and re-living the moment over and over was too painful. You can only take so much punishment in one session. Luckily, the perfect distraction is at hand. The results of the bivvy makeover were so *X-treme*, I've decided to extend the concept. Been down to B&Q to pick up a few more spray cans. This time it's the car getting the treatment. Various shades of green and brown on the front seat, for the perfect 'bivvy tramp on tour' look.

I'm well underway when I hear a voice calling me from across the car park.

"Hello there, Kes isn't it?"

"Steve, what brings you to St. Ives Boathaven."

"Everyone's talking about the St. Ives car camo artist; wondered if you could do my wagon?"

"Yeah, yeah, what do you reckon, it's the business isn't it? I'm nearly finished."

"It's different mate!"

"Only cost me a few quid."

"Yeah looks like it; not sure it'll catch on," he says laughing.

"You wait and see, Dave Lane's having his done tomorrow, then it's Terry Hearn."

"Yeah yeah, sure they're queuing down the A14 as we speak. Anyway, look, I'm trying to find a boat, for my Fen Drayton campaign. Came to see what deals they've got on inflatables and life jackets."

"I'll take you in to see the lads. They'll sort something out!"

"Cool. Have you used my weighsling and scales yet?"

"Bad timing Steve: bloody lost one this morning. Makes me sick thinking about it!"

"You need to go to a runs water, catch a few fish, put it out of your mind."

I tell Steve all about Marsh Lakes. He can't believe there will be sixty, seventy and 90-pounders swimming around less than a mile from where we're standing and asks when he can get on there. I take his mobile number and say I'll check out the situation for the opening with Harry.

"They're wrong 'uns mate," I say.

"Who cares, it's a lot cheaper than going abroad."

Twelve

A bad day's fishing is better than a good day at work.

Anon.

Shortly after 9.30am on Sunday morning; St. Ives bridge. I park up the newly painted Passat, and admire the way it reluctantly reflects the summer sunshine. The meadow looks a picture, brimful of wild flowers, cows grazing in the distance and a long line of anglers on the Hemingford bank. It's perfect Cambridgeshire countryside, meadows, willows and water, punctuated by the soaring spires of village churches. I haven't had a change of heart. Tommy asked me to lend a bit of support at the start-of-the-season fishing match. Less welcome to the scene is the small group of *FishAction* supporters waving their battle flags on the bridge. I spot Jay on the meadow taking pictures and amble down to join him. Tommy is up at the farthest peg. He looks a bit surprised to see me with Jay Johnson, but gives a wave.

"What do you reckon about this anti-angling protest then?" Jay asks an angler.

"Look mate, I don't mind them waving a few flags on the bridge, it's a free country. But it could get ugly if they come down here and disturb the fishing."

"Could be a problem then," Jay whispers, as we walk away.

"I see you're under cover then Jay!"

"Not at all, I'm here as a *FishAction* supporter, not from the *Town Crier*."

"Oh, really?"

"Yes, really. Just testing the temperature before we do anything."

"I think you're a bit outnumbered, so I wouldn't recommend any stunts. Have you got Saira on a short leash today?"

"Saira does what she pleases, as you well know."

"Yes, that's what worries me," I say.

"Me too," Jay says, smiling.

We can see Saira and her pal Danny leading the way through the Dolphin Hotel car park and out onto the lush green meadow. A row of 30 heads turn. Surprisingly, despite some severely frosty stares they reach the last peg without incident. Jay is relieved, but as they set off back down the line, Jim, a big burly geezer, stands up in his swim and shouts, "Why don't you sodding hippies piss off and leave us alone."

"Why don't you stop torturing the fish?" Saira shouts back.

Jay looks nervous, "Oh no, here we go!"

Danny, a bit further up the line, takes a large rock out of his rucksack and lobs it in the water.

"Caught anything mate?" He shouts at the angler in front of him.

It looks like the angler is going to steam into Danny, but thinks better of it when he sizes up the six foot four frame and number-one hair cut in front of him. His mate from the next swim intervenes.

"Leave it Tim, the tosser isn't worth the effort."

"Bring it on!" says Danny calmly, putting down his bag.

"OK everyone, let's head back to the bridge," says Jay. But to his obvious dismay Saira is stripping off. "Anyone fancy a swim. Lovely day for it," she says.

The anglers look confused. This extremely curvaceous young woman in a skimpy black bikini is getting ready to completely ruin their fishing match. A few of the lads seem to see the funny side of it though and are enjoying the view, while others have faces like thunder. Saira plunges into the river, making as much splash as she can muster.

"Well, get your camera out then," she shouts at Jay, "it's bloody cold in here!"

"You knew about this didn't you?" Jay hisses at Danny.

"Of course, we planned it ages ago."

"If I'd known Saira gets her kit off at these protests I'd have invited a few more friends along," I say.

Jay doesn't look impressed and concentrates on taking a few shots of the watery chaos.

"Now I know she's off her trolley!" I add.

But it isn't Saira's swim that makes the headlines. When we read about the day's events in the *Crier*, Jay's editor has put a rather different spin on the story:

Angling Protest Ends in Violence

An anti-angling protest ended in violence as scuffles broke out between anglers and members of the FishAction pressure group on Sunday, leaving one person needing hospital treatment for a suspected broken arm. Tommy Tindall of Tommy's Tackle, St. Ives said, "We've been holding regular matches here for 30 years and never had any trouble before. Our day of legal sport was deliberately ruined and several of our members' cars have been damaged. I expect the police to take action against those responsible."

FishAction have denied all allegations of criminal damage to anglers' vehicles, and Police are investigating the incident which took place around 4.00 p.m. on the old London Road in St. Ives. Saira Parsons, spokesperson for the pressure group FishAction, stated "What we have here is a mindless and totally unprovoked attack on people who were there to make a peaceful protest. Around a dozen anglers joined a frenzied attack, attempting at one point to roll the FishAction Land Rover. Luckily the driver managed to somehow get the vehicle away, as what would have happened if they had gained access to the other protestors inside doesn't bear thinking about."

In response, Tommy Tindall said, "This incident has been blown out of all proportion. Some of the lads rocked their vehicle at one point, and unfortunately in the confusion one of them was clipped by a passing car. It was an accident, and no one was physically attacked. If they hadn't deliberately ruined the fishing match then none of this would have happened. I hold them totally responsible."

The Police are continuing their investigation, and at this time no one has been charged.

Thirteen

*I had rather be a failure at something I enjoy
than be a success at something I hate.*

George F. Burns

We arrive at Marsh Lakes on Monday morning in rather glum mood. The events of the day before have taken the shine off what should have been a red letter day. Tommy's not really said much this morning, which is unusual. Ron on the other hand is wearing his emotions on his sleeve. He's out for revenge first chance he gets. As for me, the idea that anyone can be so passionately opposed to something I love has sent my moral compass spinning. But it doesn't take much to do that; I'm almost permanently confused.

"I hear you had a bit of a run in with the Bunnyhugger brigade lads. Well, I've got something that'll take your minds off that. Follow me," Harry says.

Down the lane we can see a 40ft articulated lorry parked by a large swim, and several men gathered at the back. They are speaking in what sounds like an eastern European language, which I can't exactly place. It's a bit of a surprise when Harry barks out a fluent order in their own language. The men stop and stand to one side. Peering into the gloom of the container we can make out a door at the back. Harry jumps up and invites us to follow. Beyond the door, is a small space with several large black tanks and an aeration system running from a large battery. Harry removes the lid off the nearest tank and we all peer down into the blackness. Just below the surface nestled in a soft mesh we can see the back of a very large common.

"It must be 60lb?" I say.

"Not a bad guess Kes, it's 65lb actually. Have a look at these two up here."

Harry takes the lids off the tanks.

"These are my prize fish, the two largest we're going to stock, real Euro monsters."

"I've never seen anything like it in my life," Ron splutters.

"That mirror must be 90lb," whispers Tommy, almost reverently.

"Impressive isn't she? 95lb 12oz when we put her in there."

"You weren't kidding when you said monsters Harry."

"Did you think I was bullshitting Tommy? I always say what I mean – and mean what I say!"

"When do they go into the lake Mr Plant, I'd love to see that?" I say.

"You can call me Harry; we're business partners now. They're going in today, that's why I invited you all over, wanted you to see them with your own eyes."

"It's the real deal!" Tommy says, winking at me.

"No wonder you've got razor wire and cameras all over the place. These are the biggest fish in England," I say.

"I've got swipe cards for you all, so you can come and go as you please. They're all individually coded, and linked to a clever bit of software, so I can check who's coming in and out. Plenty of thieving scumbags around."

I'm staring straight at Harry, but can't see one bit of irony on his face. He clearly doesn't see himself as a thieving scumbag. Maybe I've got him all wrong. Maybe it is all above board.

"The other day I totally forgot to ask when the lakes will open," Tommy says.

"If we can get all the fish stocked by the end of June, we'll open for business at the beginning of August. I want to give them at least a month to settle down."

"They could get a bit of a hammering," I say.

"Won't happen. If one fish keeps coming out, I'll stick it in the stock pond, till things quieten down, then put it back in for the winter. And if they're coming out left, right and centre, I'll shut the lake down for a few weeks."

"Glad to hear it Harry," Ron says.

"I'm not so worried about the other two lakes, but the Monsters Lake stock are the crown jewels; got to treat them like royalty."

Outside one of Harry's men is arranging a mat, weighsling and camera on a tripod in one of the swims. Harry says something to him in the foreign language and he nods without smiling.

"What's that language you're speaking Harry?" Tommy asks.

"Hungarian; my man Istvan runs a fish farm out there, and helped me source the fish I was after."

"How did you learn to speak it so fluently Harry?" I ask.

"Always got a question this lad," says Harry winking at Tommy, "nosey bastard aren't ya? If you must know, my old dear was from Hungary. Came over as a kid after the war and married dad. Anyway, enough questions, I'm just going up the house to get changed and then we can have a proper look at the fish. Ron, come up with me, I'd like a word?"

Harry walks with Ron back up to the house. Tommy and I take the opportunity to stroll around the lakes.

"What do you think Kes, should I go for it?"

"Tricky, could be a one way ticket to Troublesville! It looks good on the surface, but check out the heavy-looking foreign dudes, and that lorry with the false end to it. I'd get a contract if I were you."

"You're right. I've been so blown away by the whole idea I haven't focused on the risks."

"But the fish, my God, the fish Tommy. Have you ever seen anything like it?"

"Only in Carpworld mate. Never thought we'd see fish like that round here."

"He's going to have people queuing down the A14 for a ticket."

"Kes, I haven't told you but Tommy's Tackle is badly in the red. I can't see it lasting; this feels like my only chance."

"Shit, I didn't think it had got that bad. You think you might roll the dice on this one?"

"I'm still nervous. Why has he chosen us?"

"No idea, whole thing seems a bit odd, but I think this is a hobby for him. He said he's not interested in being a shop keeper, and he certainly doesn't look like he needs the money."

Ron emerges about 20 minutes later and joins us on the lawn overlooking the Monsters Lake.

"You look like the boy whose dad bought a sweet shop," Tommy says.

"Not quite, but it went well."

"Did he give you a gun?" I ask.

"Very funny, Kes!"

"Well, I assume you're his new gamekeeper, and you've already got a Barbour and a flat cap," I say whipping Ron's hat and donning it myself at a jaunty angle.

"Not gamekeeper, bailiff, and give my hat back," Ron says, smiling but grabbing my arm, putting it behind my back and squeezing until I shout submit.

"Kes thinks Harry is some kind of gangster," Tommy says.

"Bullshit; just a businessman, smuggling a few fish into the country."

"And that doesn't make you nervous?" I ask, pretending Ron has really hurt my arm.

"Can't see the harm in it myself, and stop that you tart there's nothing wrong with your arm. If I wanted to hurt you I would have."

"See! Look, he's only been working for Harry for two minutes and he's already assaulted me."

"*Tart!*" Ron mouths in my direction.

"So you think we should grab it with both hands?" Tommy asks.

"Too right! We'd be mugs to pass it up!" Ron says.

"What did he ask you about then?"

"A bit about my family and whether I had any experience dealing with trouble. Told him about my days as a bouncer in Huntingdon, and he seemed quite happy that I'd done some amateur boxing as a youngster. The money's crap, but I get to fish whenever I like. Oh, and Kes, he's paying for me to get a shotgun licence."

"See, told you; bet it's a sawn off," I say.

Harry comes strolling down the lawn in camo chest waders and a pink pin-striped shirt with the sleeves rolled up. We all look at each other and smile. We're not sure quite what to make of our carping sugar daddy, but he's certainly made a big impression on us in a very short space of time. Whatever my concerns, I can't help thinking he's got it made. Drop dead gorgeous wife, massive house, every bit of fishing kit you could ever want, and the biggest carp in England in his back garden. Not bad for a bloke who recycles rubbish.

"OK lads let's get those beauties out and have a good look before we put them in their new home."

Istvan and one of the other Hungarians bring the first of the fish out to the back of the trailer in a black sack. They stand on the loading lift, holding the fish with long poles over their shoulders and one hand each under its belly. Even in the sack it looks massive. They carefully lower the fish down onto the mat, and undo the sack. I am worried that they'll be rough with it, but it's clear these guys are used to handling big lumps. And what a whacker it is, the big common, its silvery flanks dazzling us in the morning sun. It clearly hasn't seen much action, as the mouth, fins and scales are mint. It's not the longest of fish, but very deep in the body, and incredibly wide across the back.

The next fish is even more gobsmacking. It weighs in at 71lb, a lovely dark mirror with big apple-slice scales scattered along its lateral line. But even this beast is put in the shade by the final leviathan. We all gasp in awe and wonder as Istvan reveals one of the biggest carp on the planet.

"Mucho mucho gigantic," I say, which gets a laugh from everyone, even Istvan.

She's long with deep grey sides, truly massive in frame, almost a leather but with a cluster of scales around the wrist of the tail. She sends the scales spinning round to 43kg, or in old money 95lb, just slightly down on what she weighed when she left Hungary. It sounds stupid to say, but it looks like she could grow even bigger. It definitely feels weird – and frankly not right – that in the near future Harry could have the world record carp swimming around at the bottom of his garden, in Fenstanton.

My own fishing has improved since I relaxed the rigid specimen hunter
approach that once motivated me. Now I can warmly congratulate a
friend who has banked a good fish and really mean it.

George Sharman, *Carp and the Carp Angler*, 1980

t's been a strange week in the shop; the place is suddenly the centre of attention again. Old and new faces are popping in on the pretence of buying a few bits, but really to get the gossip on both the action at the match last Sunday and the news spreading like wildfire along the carping bush telegraph that a new and special complex is about to open. By the time Sunday morning rolls round I'm glad to have a day away from it; a day off from the shop, but not a day off from the boot sale and the quest for all things carpy.

Over the years I've scooped some rare and precious car booty. I'm always on the lookout for anything carp related, but have a special weakness for carp books and magazines. Yes, despite what Ron and Tommy say, I can read and enjoy tracing the history of our glorious sport. My greatest achievement to date was a mint 1972 first edition of *Quest for Carp* by Jack Hilton. Hidden at the bottom of a box full of romances, it was received into my shaking hands like the Holy Grail. No not that one, I mean a first edition of *The Compleat Angler*. Fully prepared to give the woman every pound in my pocket, I was left reeling by the price tag of 50p, a truly euphoric moment in my bootnik career.

I like to think of myself as a car boot predator, with a clear prey image, and ruthlessly efficient foraging strategy. Pacing slowly up the aisles, head moving from side to side scanning for boxes of books, I stop and scan the horizon for rods pointing skywards. Nothing, head back down for the books. Slipping through the early morning crowd, I'm beginning to think it will be a blank day, when suddenly, treasure. Don't panic, adrenaline surging, eyes sending incredible signals to spinning brain, this is it! There on the ground, laid out for all to see, is virtually every carp book worth having. "I'm in!", pinching myself to check I'm not still in the land of nod back at the Lagoon.

"How much are these books?" I ask as calmly as possible, somewhat giving the game away by simultaneously gathering up as many as I can manage.

"Make me an offer; I just want to get rid of them."

I do a quick calculation, my pulse racing. 'The Carp Strikes Back', 'Casting at the Sun', 'Tiger Bay', 'In Pursuit of the Largest', 'Redmire Pool': I'm thinking, *"There must be £500 worth here at least"*, but I say, "How about a £100 for the lot?"

"I'll take £20."

"Bloody hell, I thought you were supposed to get me to raise my price?"

Poor cow; husband's probably crocked it and she's a bit confused. Doesn't have a clue what she's got.

"I'd feel like I nicked them."

"Alright give me £50 for them. If you don't want them, I'll sell to someone else."

"How come you're selling them anyway, it's a nice collection?"

"I'm sick of fishing. He's away in France at the moment. And even when he is here, it's either preparing for fishing, fishing, or down the lake talking about fishing."

"Bit of a carp widow are you? Well at least he's not down the pub."

"Oh if only that were true dear. No, he's in for a right shock when he gets back. Hopefully it will bring him to his senses. I'm not running a bloody hotel anymore."

I hand over a £50 note and gather up my haul to end all hauls.

"What have you got there?" Ron asks as I walk past the beach back at the Lagoon.

"Don't tell me, you're moving into that swim, or have you just bought a whole load of Jack Charlton's books?"

"I've just had a very bizarre haul down at the boot sale. Look at this lot. I'm feeling a bit guilty; bloke's wife was flogging them off while he's away fishing, to teach him a lesson."

"Poor bastard, must have taken him years to collect this lot."

"Yeah, if we find out who they belong to I'll have to sell them back to him."

After getting the rods back out in Fatty's I sprawl out on the bedchair, one eye on the amazing box of books, the other on my lifeless swim. *"Mmmm, top five carp books of all time".* Have I got them all in that box I wonder, pulling it beside me? The first one that comes to hand is certainly a contender for a top five berth, a 1977 second impression of *Quest for Carp*. Jack Hilton was the master of big carp captures back in the late '60s and early '70s. Ashlea Pool and Redmire were happy hunting grounds for this hero of the sport. Next one that comes out is *Tiger Bay*. Well it's a cracking read, but maybe *Bazil's Bush* would be Rob Maylin's contribution. *Carp Sense*, by Jim Gibbinson, *The Complete Carper* by Andy Little and *Carp Fishing* by Tim Paisley, all classic titles. What else have we got in here? Ah yes, now we're definitely talking top five, for pure quality of the captures within its covers, *In Pursuit of the Largest* by the main man Mr Hearn. Here's another favourite, *Carp and the Carp Angler*, George Sharman.

What makes a classic carp book? I stare up through the leaves searching for inspiration. That's it, *inspiration*. It has to have some awesome captures in it, to set the pulse racing and the imagination soaring. Does it have to be well written? It helps. Dad reckoned Chris Yates was the master wordsmith, conjuring up choice words to capture the true spirit of our noble art. I reckon he's a bit old school for the twenty first century, but he's still a magician with the pen. Yatesy totally gets it, and you can't argue with a man who caught the Bishop, Britain's first 50-pounder. I like to think of him as a Jedi Knight, guarding the force. Yeah that's it, Chris Yates is our Obi-Wan Kenobi. Here it is, *Casting at the Sun*, a classic, on the pile it goes. While we're talking old school, I suppose Ron would say BB's *Confessions of a Carp Fisher*. Well, it's a good title, and some lovely stuff about the trials and tribulations of the lifelong carp addict. Next out of the box, is *Carp Fever*. Yes, no question. First modern technical carp book; Hair rig, baits, winter carp fishing, and a chapter by Peter Springate: enough said, it's on the pile. And that's another criterion, technical information; I do like a good technical book. But I'm sure you'll agree, a good carp book must have gripping fishy tales, and there's no one who can spin an entertaining yarn better than Rod. Here it is, the next one for the list, *The Carp Strikes Back*. Right then, let's see. I lay out my top five on the ground beside me for further consideration; yes happy with that:

1) *Carp Strikes Back* – Rod Hutchinson
2) *In Pursuit of the Largest* – Terry Hearn
3) *Carp Fever* – Kevin Maddocks
4) *Casting at the Sun* – Chris Yates
5) *Bazil's Bush* – Rob Maylin

Not bad, I wish the fishing was as satisfying. I've got that blanking feeling, and pull the line on my right-hand rod, just to reassure myself that someone hasn't superglued my bobbins to the ground.

"Ah, so you can move, feel free to do it any time, and preferably this month."

Talking to your bobbins is generally mocked, even amongst desperate Lagooners. In contrast, walking up the bank 50m is always considered worth a try, and a practice religiously observed by many. Another of my take-inducing tactics is to turn the buzzers off and crank up the iPod. This morning I've tried them all without success. Not having caught a carp for three months is taking its toll on my confidence and enthusiasm. At these times I try to put my old school motto into practice, *Do different*! It had always seemed a bit bloody odd, but applied to carp fishing I finally saw what Mr Hebditch was banging on about in those dreary assemblies. "*Right then, if they're not feeding on the bottom, or the top, then maybe they're hanging about in midwater. Maybe I'll try a Zig rig for a few hours.*"

The birds have been driving me nuts; not that kind, seagulls and their other feathered cousins. Shouldn't we rename the little buggers, lakegulls or baitgulls? They seem to spend all their time hanging around miles from the sea these days, annoying the hell out of carp anglers. Seagulls have an amazing ability for spotting an airborne boilie. You sit for hours with no sign of the marine raiders, open your bait box, reach for your catapult and there they are, swooping and squawking, plunging head first into your swim. Fishing in four feet of water off the old island there's also been a bit of coot action, but nothing a few choice pebbles across the beak haven't sorted out. Finally I settle back into my bedchair happy that everything is pukka, the new balanced-hook rigs primed and ready for impact. I am soon pushing out the Zs, enjoying a Sunday morning snooze, dreaming of the Lady.

The left-hand buzzer bursts into life, a piercing one-noter shattering the Sunday morning calm. Falling off my bedchair I stumble to the rod bouncing in its rest, but register something moving over the baited area, "*Oh please no, not a bloody swan.*" Picking up the rod it's clear this is not the wildlife encounter I had hoped for. "*Please let the hook come out.*" I open the bale arm and the swan settles down, but the rig is hanging from its beak. "*Shit, Shit, Shit; you stupid bastard!*" I'm not sure if I mean me, or the bird.

At that moment Ron appears at my shoulder.

"Having fun? I thought you were fishing, not wildfowling."

"Very funny Ron. What am I going to do?"

"Well, you'd better ring the Queen first; you've just hooked one of her birds."

"This is a nightmare!"

"Don't worry my old son, I'll deal with it. I used to ring them down at Huntingdon. They're all right so long as you're calm and firm. You don't want 'em flapping all over the place; complete chaos that is. Tighten up to her and then wind slowly"

The swan feels surprisingly light on 70m of X-line. With its head down low and wings tucked back, it slips easily across the surface.

"That's it, keep her coming".

Ron wades in up to his knees. The swan seems to know what's coming. Rearing up on its arse, hissing and spreading its impressive and frightening wings, it whips the water to a froth, soaking Ron and scaring the shit out of me. Undeterred Ron lunges forward and grabs the swan by its neck with his left hand and wrestles it under his right arm.

"Right Kes, get this hook out."

The size 6 is lodged in its bottom beak, but a firm pull with the forceps sets it free. Ron lowers the swan gently back onto the water, and the magnificent bird drifts away, glancing back at us and somehow looking distinctly annoyed and threatening.

"Thanks Ron, I don't think I could have dealt with that myself."

"Those yellow boilies seem to be real bird magnets; you should wear one round your neck."

"I tell you what, I won't be fishing the margins for a while and I'm going over to barbless hooks."

"Don't be an arse Kes, you don't want to sit on here for months and have the hook fall out at the net. Just stick to fishing singles on the shallow spots at night."

Lesson learnt!

There is no complete happiness without complete idleness.

Anton Chekhov

have a reputation for, as Ron calls it, 'going off on one'; meandering down the less travelled parts of my brain. He likes to call me a mentalist. I call it *X-treme thinking*. I'm not one for charging round a football pitch, climbing up mountains and the like, but I'm pretty keen on giving my brains a good workout. Carp fishing and thinking were made for each other. Hours of sitting around, punctuated by a few minutes of frantic activity leaves plenty of quality thinking time available. Being a recently promoted camper, the pressure is mounting to justify this self-appointed accolade, so I'm trying to suss out what I need to work on, what separates carpers from campers.

Every month articles are published about improving catches by being 'in tune with a water'. Being naturally down to earth types, we like to call it watercraft, something that can be learned through apprenticeship. More of a City and Guilds course than a Doctorate in Philosophy. But can you learn this stuff? Are some people just naturally gifted in this department, and the rest of us kidding ourselves? You read about the top anglers feeling inexplicably confident, in the zone, their natural hunting instincts honed to a state of high alert. When they feel, not think, what is right. Maybe, but I think you can learn the basics. I'm not blessed with natural angling instincts. I can't look at a water and read it immediately, know where and how to approach it, see the patterns, the best spots, the right line angles, the rig that will give the best presentation. But what I do have in my armoury are my thinking skills. I can, slowly, painfully slowly, work my way through the jigsaw and make a reasonable stab at putting the pieces together.

The bad news for newbies is there aren't too many short cuts to gaining your watercraft wings. You have to get out there and chalk up the experiences. It's what sorts out the instant carpers – or, as Ron likes to say, *"Those with all the gear, but no idea."* – from those who've served their apprenticeship. Another of Ron's sayings that stuck with me is *"Some people have ten years' experience, and others have one year's experience repeated ten times."*

I've been carp fishing for 12 years, but don't have 12 years' experience. I wasn't paying attention for the first six, and have been a bit distracted by girls, music and chemical stimulants for the last four. So although I've done a lot of rod hours and been around for a while, I've still got plenty to learn. And it seems the more you learn the more you realise what you don't know. There are so many pieces in this carp fishing jigsaw, and every day you find someone has been along in the night, mixed up the pieces again and even changed the final picture. I suppose that's what makes it endlessly fascinating and challenging.

How much of your fishing is an act of faith and how much is based on knowledge? I think the campers are often working on faith and belief rather than knowledge. The top anglers do everything they can to ensure they know they're fishing effectively. They can then endure the long periods of waiting, part of life on waters like the Lagoon, confident they are not wasting their time. It's not so easy for the rest of us. Take the other day for instance. I was perfectly focused on placing a couple of bags up against the old lake island, when it suddenly occurred to me that I had no way of being certain that my baits were in A1 position. Previous experience gave me confidence that they would be, but ultimately it was an act of faith that something wasn't fatally wrong with the presentation that would render the whole exercise futile. Unluckily for Tommy, he happened to arrive in the swim at that very moment.

"Tommy, how do you know you're not wasting your time?"

"Here we go. What do you mean exactly, wasting my time generally in life or specifically down at the Lagoon. Cos you know we're mostly camping down here."

"I was just thinking that casting is like an act of faith; you don't know that everything is pukka, but you have to believe it is. If you don't, then it's impossible to sit hour after hour waiting!"

"Yeah, whatever Kes!"

"Don't be like that, it's not bullshit, we really have to believe that we are fishing effectively to fish effectively," I plead.

"Well, I like to drop a new rig in the margins and try casting it a few times and if it doesn't tangle and looks OK, then that's good enough for me. I'll fish it and be confident."

"So you are a man of science, you like to test and gather evidence, and this is your way of knowing you are fishing effectively. My problem philosophically, is that just because the sun has risen in the east every day of my life doesn't mean that it will rise in the east tomorrow. And my next cast could tangle so how can I sit there confidently?"

"Your problem Kes, as Ron and I have told you on more than one occasion, is that you are full of shite, and think too much!"

"Of course that may or may not be true, but we have no way of knowing for sure. I rest my case. We must resort to belief in many of the big questions of life."

"Kes, you nut job, whether your rig is tangled is not up there with, 'Where do we come from? Is there a God? Or is there life on Mars?' Why don't you leave the philosophy to those boffins down the A14 in Cambridge?"

"Oh it's far too important to leave it in their hands. We are all equal in our infinite ignorance!"

"I don't know where you get them from Kes, but you keep us all entertained."

"That's cool!"

"The question is, are you going to leave those baits in position?" Tommy asks.

"The question is, should I?"

"I'm off mate; you shouldn't reason with the mentally insane, it's a bottomless pit"

"Very good Tommy, you're getting the hang of this philosophy lark!"

The baits, in position all night, were not tangled when I reeled in. The mental torture continues.

"Morning Tommy, morning Ron." I say, ambling in from the Islands swim next door. "The good news is I think I've been fishing effectively all night. The bad news is the carp didn't notice, or rather did notice, or whatever. The point is I'm still blanking, but I don't think it's my presentation, but then again I'm not sure about that."

"Kes, it's 8 o'clock in the morning, you'll fry your brains if you don't give them a rest now and then," Tommy says.

"I'm afraid it's too late for that, I've been fiddling around since six. May I present Kes's latest kipper-catching contraption. Observe, 10cm of braid, a hinged link swivel and 5cm of fluorocarbon. Pretty standard Stiff rig stuff you may say, but the cunning part is the hook. I've been racking my brains on how to improve the hooking efficiency with bottom baits."

Glued to the shank of this wide gape long shank size four hook is a length of black foam. "When I place it in the water it sits up, the point perfectly placed to catch the bottom lip." I pull the rig through the water and then drag it forward like it has been sucked in by a big old *Cypry*.

"Observe, if you will gents, the position of the hook and imagine its trajectory into the gob of a very hungry or even mildly curious scaly lump. I think you'll agree that said 'floating hook' would go into the mouth point down."

"And because of the stiff fluoro, it's a bit of a tricky one to spit out," Tommy says.

"The theory being that the stiffness of the link means it can't flip over on the way out," I add.

"And the blighter is nailed in the bottom lip," Ron says.

"Well I never, this one could actually work," Tommy says.

"I know, I can't quite believe it myself. I suppose it's a variation on the lead shot rig, but it just sits so perfectly and being buoyant, even size four hooks will be sucked in with virtually no resistance. Fantastic hooking potential without the drawbacks of big heavy hooks".

"But you will need to use big baits, so that the carp really have to open their mouths."

"A big bait but with nearly neutral buoyancy is what we need. We're back to my obsession with luncheon meat," I say. "What do you think Ron?"

"It all sounds great, Kes, but I think you'll find that Andy Little got there first. I seem to remember something similar in his book *The Complete Carp Angler,* but it wasn't exactly the same. There are plenty of fabulous rigs dreamt up in sleeping bags; the real test is whether it actually catches fish."

"Yeah, thanks for the cold water mate. I can always rely on you to bring me down."

"Sorry Kes, it does look like it might work."

We drop the subject and turn our attention to tea, the weather and the whereabouts of her Ladyship, all the really important things in a Lagoon bivvy tramp's life.

Sixteen

No man who is occupied in doing a very difficult thing,
and doing it very well, ever loses his self-respect.

George Bernard Shaw

After the disappointment of losing a fish last week, I'm desperate for the next chance. Surveillance has been stepped up, walking round and round each day trying to work out patterns to the shows (or, rather, making up patterns and theories as some small comfort to the Lagoon punishment). Yesterday, my luck turned; I found a few fish milling around the reeds in the southwest corner, and hallelujah, they were feeding hard on a margin spot. I haven't heard about anyone baiting it, or seen anyone fishing it, so went ahead and put in a kilo of the Monster Crab boilies yesterday evening. Could hardly sleep last night, thinking I should have got straight in there, but it's a tricky swim to fish and not one that people usually bivvy up in. All the same I was still imagining rods poking out of the reeds as I came along at first light. But no, all quiet, no sign of life anywhere, on the bank or in the water. Hopefully the fish will return once the sun comes up over the rock-crushing plant.

Stepping into the drink, the boots of my chest waders send silt billowing into the reeds. Gingerly I take another step, anxious to avoid a big cloud drifting out into the swim. I love getting in the water; the connection immediately puts me in the zone, and the precision of lowering your bait onto a spot gives ultimate confidence. The area looks nice and clear with no sign of my bait from yesterday. *They're on it, or the birds are!* The reeds extend out about three metres at this point, shelving away deeper than I can make in my waders. With Polaroids on I can see a few perch milling around. *SHIT!* A hefty mirror comes ambling along the reed line. I daren't breathe or even move my eyes. We're literally ten feet from each other. She has slowed right down, and I'm sure the next movement will be a quick flick of her tail as she bolts away. But amazingly she seems to be preoccupied with examining her new larder, and slowly hoovers a line diagonally away from me. *Oh My God! Don't do anything, just keep absolutely still!*

After what seems like several hours, but is only about 30 seconds, she drifts off into deep water. I seize my opportunity, carefully lower the new 'floating hook' rig into position, and slip a back lead on for good measure. I'm buzzing; this could be it. I decide it's a one-rod chance, so all I can do now is sit back and wait. It may sound strange for a carper to say this, but I find it hard to just sit back and do nothing. I like to be active, tying rigs, priming spots, getting up trees, so have to work hard at being patient and still. I can do it, but just have to remind myself to relax, sit back and enjoy time spent by the water. As Mr Walton himself instructed, "*Study to be quiet.*"

The swim is tight, no room for luxuries like brollies or chairs. I lie back on my unhooking mat and stare up through the branches of an old alder. A robin is staring back down at me, chirping his warning call for all he's worth.

"Yeah Yeah, I know it's your manor, but you'll just have to put up with me for a few hours."

Talking to birds, even if only of the feathered variety, is a good way to pass the time, and robins are particularly good company. This little fella is clearly in no mood to share his prime real estate, and tries to scare me off with a couple of daring flights low over my head.

"Will you give it a rest, there's a big carp out there havin' its breakfast and I'm going nowhere."

I try to make the peace by crumbling a few boilies for him. This seems to do the trick, as he immediately flutters down for a nosh.

"Happy now?" Apparently we are now friends, because the cheeky little chap hops right onto the toe of my left boot, and cocks his head this way and that, as if to say *any chance of a bit more mate?*

I'm really trying to lie still, enjoy the morning, and wait for something to happen. I know this is by far the best thing to do, that any movements could ruin my chance. But, I just have to know what's going on, and carefully get to my feet to peer down into the swim. *Whoops!* A big dark shape, slap bang over the spot. *Better just sit back down. It's going to happen*! I stare at my rod, looking for any tell-tale twitching from the limp braid as it enters the water. Nothing, the back lead is doing its job. Out beyond the reeds there is a definite boil on the surface, as my guest troughs her way around the breakfast menu of Monster Crab served with a few handfuls of hemp. *Go on baby, you know you want it!*

Ten minutes have passed and I'm still in limbo; time for another look. No sign of life. *Maybe something is wrong. Should I move the rig? Should I double my chances by putting in another rod? Has she spooked and left for the day? Oh please let this be the chance I've been waiting for.* I have to do something, so opt for sitting a bit further back, reasoning that the pressure you feel is inversely related to the distance you are from the action. Doubling the distance from your rods halves the tension you feel. I can see Ron coming up the track, and, panic stricken about his big plodding feet, start waving my hands trying to communicate the delicate nature of my predicament. This confuses Ron and he breaks into a run. *Oh shit!* I tip toe toward him at top speed, waving even more frantically.

"Are you alright, I thought you were in trouble mate?"

"Fish... on my spot... margin!"

"Oh I see, Lagoon yips, eh?"

"Bad Ron, very bad."

We sit down and Ron tries to take my mind off the present by launching into one of his very long stories about free-lining in the '70s. It works because when the inevitable scream comes from my *Micron EOS* it takes a couple of seconds to register that it's calling me.

"Go on son, go get her."

Somewhere deep in my brain I register that Ron said *her*, that it could be the Lady.

"Feels like a lump" I say, rod arched over, braid ticking steadily off the spool.

"They're all lumps."

Ron's right, this is not a pasty-commons venue. And being a relative newbie in these circles, the doubts creep in, *Did I check those knots this morning? Err no. What a plonker!* She seems very determined to get down the left-hand margin.

"Are there any snags down there?" I ask nervously.

"No, but it's pretty weedy all the way round."

With that everything goes still and solid. I don't do anything for a minute or so, hoping that she will make the first move.

"I think she's off!"

"Rubbish, be patient. Wait a couple of minutes then give it the butt end. The pressure will get her moving again."

I decide to give her some slack.

"What are you doing, don't give her an inch. You'll lose it for sure if you wimp out."

I lean back and exert as much pressure as I dare, all the while thinking these are shit or bust tactics.

"I think I felt something." A slight judder down the line then, unmistakably, a movement on the other end. "Yes, she's still on."

"Told you didn't I? Works a treat with the braid. Now bully her up this way."

I try but the fish has other plans and uses her bulk to kite out in front of me.

At last I feel a bit more in control, but am still totally convinced it will all end in disaster.

"Don't rush it Kes. You're in charge now. Keep her on a short line and let her tire herself out."

Ron, bless him, joins me in the water, stripped down to his underpants. It's not a sight for those of a nervous disposition, but he's oblivious to the public decency offence, totally focused with net in hand. *Don't you just love the big fella!*

My nerves are shredded as she rolls over the braid. But it's her final move. A big white underbelly and gasping mouth signal surrender. I draw her the final few yards across the surface and Ron lifts the net cord.

"Get in there you beauty," Ron says.

"Monster!" I shout.

"Congratulations Kes, you're no longer a Lagoon virgin!"

We're joined by a few of the other Lagooners. This is still a rare enough occasion that everyone wants to feel the magic and feast their eyes on one of the elusive scaly beasts. As usual I'm in a right state, but am concentrating intensely for fear of making an elementary mistake and revealing my newbie status in front of this lofty and – let's face it – critical company. Everything is set, and I haul the sack out of the margin.

"A good 30 by the looks of it."

"Nah, big 20 I reckon," says someone else.

The dial spins round and settles at 34lb 12oz.

"Well done Kes, that's a real cracker," Ron says.

"Good angling Kes," Tommy, who has just arrived, says. "Shame it's a poached fish!"

"What do you mean?" I ask, feeling a bit annoyed and anxious that Tommy of all people is having a pop at me in public.

"Well, I've been baiting this corner for the last couple of weeks. And you've managed to nip in and nick one off my spot."

"You kept that quiet Tommy," Ron says. "You can't expect people to ignore feeding fish if you don't let on it's your bait they're munching on."

"Relax boy's, you're right, it's my own fault for not telling you. Let's get some great shots of Kes' new PB."

I have to admit that it took a bit of the shine off the capture, but it was still a magic moment in my Lagoon adventure, and given the number of campaigns people are running on the lake, it's almost inevitable that you'll be treading on someone's toes when you move onto feeding fish.

Part Two

And gentlemen in England now a-bed
Shall think themselves accurs'd they were not here,
And hold their manhoods cheap whiles any speaks
That fought with us upon Saint Crispin's day!

William Shakespeare, Henry V, 1599

Seventeen

He who dares, wins!

Winston Churchill

battle is won, but the war goes on. I'm finally off the mark, my first Lagoon fish in the bag, a notch on my bedchair. All that hard graft rewarded, and the *floating hook* rig actually works. The euphoria has seeded an idea in my spinning mind, the *X-treme Carping Club*. A club for those who actually seek out head banging waters, who have the mental toughness to fish whole seasons knowing the chances of a bite are slim. Who can hold onto the dream through blank after blank, enjoying the challenge. It's a carping philosophy, a code of the road, an *X-treme* approach to our glorious sport. At the moment membership stands at one, me. Can you have a club with a membership of one? Or is that delusional behaviour, and actually a mental health issue? Anyway, I reckon I could be onto something with this one. I'll write to Peter Springate, first choice for honorary life president! The original *X-treme carper!*

I can see it now, first a secret website, somewhere for *X-treme carpers* to commune. Like our brethren in the free climbing world, with their bible of extreme ascents, we'll compile a list of the most *X-treme* waters, places where the faint hearted fear to cast. Oh yes, it's exclusive and elitist, only the most head banging mentalists need apply. That's how we'll build our fearsome reputation. Five years on a 500 hundred acre water for five fish, that kind of thing. We'll work our way through the toughest waters in England, pioneer new approaches, and then head off into Europe. We'll dress in black hoodies, fly skull and crossbone flags from our black bivvies, drive beaten up black VW vans. We're dark and dangerous to know. We'll lead you completely astray. Forget what you had planned for this life, we're gonna fish hard and die young. Life really is too short for *X-treme carping* but we're gonna do it anyway and **** the consequences.

We're cyber carpers, fiercely independent and solitary animals, but wired and networked to fish and live as one. We are the carping Borg! You know like in Star Trek, we submit to cybernetic enhancement as a means of acheiving perfection. Well, something like that anyway. Gathering occasionally on remote waters to observe secret customs, share the knowledge, and re-affirm our lifelong commitment to a life on the edge. We'll have a black mark tattooed on the inside of our wrists, the *X-treme* carpers black mirror. This is no ordinary tattoo. It has to be done in Wisbech, using a special kind of ink, by one particular artist. We don't want any fakers passing themselves off as one of us. Once you've been screened, and the basics seem to be in place, new recruits have to prove themselves in the initiation test. This is a fearsome rite of passage, designed to test an angler's nerve, toughness, commitment and skill. You have to fish 60 nights from the beginning of January until the end of March, on a selection of up to five waters decided by a panel of founding brothers. You then have the choice to focus on one or more, in order to pass the test. Success is catching a fish from one of these *X-treme* waters in winter conditions. If you stick it out for sixty nights, but blank, you have the chance to apply again and do the test the following year. If you blank and fail to do the 60 nights, you are history, a lightweight, cast aside forever!

This is a radical shake up for the 21st century, 400 years since Izaak wrote the *Compleat Angler, it's* time for a new angling bible. We won't write it down though, the true spirit, culture and knowledge of *X-treme* carping can only be stored in our hearts and minds. Eventually, to combat the growing rumours, fear and misinformation surrounding our activities, we'll produce a DVD, giving the angling world an insight into the techniques employed to achieve our staggering results, and capturing some of the greatest *X-treme* adventures on video. *Secret Weapons for the Modern Carper* will be the cult video of the decade.

Yeah I know, alarm bells are starting to ring all over the place, this is turning into just another way to screw money out of anglers. We're selling out brothers! Internal strife, splinter groups will form like the *Original X-treme Anglers*, the *East Anglian X-treme Carping Chapter*, the *X-treme Carp Collective*. It was a cool idea while it lasted. I have plenty of cool ideas, but that's usually where they stay, tucked away in the vault, for a rainy day when I might actually have to do something cool, rather than just talk and think about it. Anyway, who am I kidding, *X-treme Carper*, x-treme bullshitter more like. I'm a million miles from mixing it with the likes of Peter Springate and Terry Hearn. But what the hell, I can't help dreaming of a day when I'm putting all the pieces together on a regular basis, truly a carper not a camper. Wanting to get there is the first step, and I want it bad.

I'm back down the Lagoon for a day and a night. Tommy, top man, could tell I needed to be here, so he gave me 24 hours. I'm set up in the nature reserve, not Tommy's spot in the corner of the old lake, and fishing a channel in the weed about 20 yards out. It doesn't look like much, but I know for a fact the Lady has been caught twice from here in the last couple of years. It just seems to be a regular patrol route, and somewhere she's happy to have a trough. I'm praying my luck's in and she's got a taste for the new Kes wonder baits. Although I should be, I have to confess to not being totally focused on the fishing.

"Hey Tommy, come over here, you're just in time to star in my new show."

"What the hell are you going on about now?"

"I've got my very own angling show. The wonders of mobile technology mean I can now provide live action straight from my bivvy."

"Oh may the lord protect me from this gibbering fool. Live action from your bivvy, sounds well dodgy."

"Very funny, not. I'm wired to the world here. Blimey, with friends like you..."

"Who said I was your friend laughing boy. Surely you know I'm paid by social services to keep an eye on you."

"Yeah, I know care in the community and all that."

"Go on then, what's on your programme?"

"I've set up a website with a live bivvycam. It's a stream of consciousness, as it all happens."

"As it happens, more like as it doesn't happen. You spanner, who on earth is going to sit around listening to you twittering on about god knows what?"

"Oh ye of little faith. It's the next big thing! You are in the presence of the Bivvy Tramp, webcasting live at BivvyTramps.co.uk."

"You've lost the plot again!"

"Sit back and watch the sponsors roll in, they'll be queuing out the back of my swim.

Once Sky Sports get wind of it I'll be signed up for a weekly show. Rob Hughes, Matt Hayes move over, make way for a real fishing superstar."

"Supertramp wrote a song in 1974 all about you Kes. Dreamer, he's nothing but a dreamer, can you see the knob on his head, oh yes, he's just a little DREAMER!" Tommy sings.

"Oh that's nice!"

"You're welcome, I've just given you your theme tune. Anyway, I haven't got time to stand around watching you make a tit of yourself."

"You'll be begging me to advertise Marsh Lakes on here in a few weeks," I shout as he walks across the car park.

Tommy takes a dim view of anglers who spend their time sitting in deluxe bivvies on their king size bedchairs watching DVDs, chatting online, in fact, doing anything except concentrating on their fishing and enjoying just being there. Tommy's basically a Luddite when it comes to computers in your swim. He's so out of touch, things have changed, the next generation of carpers are wireless wonder kids, they rip, mash and post content on the net. *YouTube* paved the way, you don't need big production crews, just a bivvy cam and something to show or say. It's so instant. Have an idea and get it out to the world. Of course there are downsides, any old numpty can have their say, just check out the forums to see how much crap people can talk. But it's the price we have to pay for freedom of expression. All hail Tim Berners-Lee! Of course THEY don't like it, people talking to each other, something outside their control. Watch out for the laws, the censorship, international corporations and governments extending their icy hand over our right to communicate and form groups across political boundaries, it's coming! Sorry, went off on one, where was I?

"Hi everyone, welcome to the first ever Bivvy Tramp blog. Today we're going to be talking about customizing your bivvy, showing you how to make a wicked chilli con carne on the bank, and giving you the latest updates on who's caught what down the Ouse valley." I pan the camera round onto the Lagoon. "As you can see we're webcasting live from St. Ives Lagoon today, and I'm bivvied up for a night in the Reserve swim. A couple of days ago I managed my first Lagoon fish, a cracking 34lb mirror, so I'm buzzing as you can imagine. Her ladyship has yet to make an appearance on the bank this year, so she's well overdue. It's midweek and the place is packed. Seems like everyone thinks she's going to do a bite real soon. I've got some pretty serious company today with Jon Mcallister opposite on the Lawns and Dave Moore down on the beach. A little bit intimidating I can tell you. Fortunately I'm not fishing too far out, so it was pretty easy to get the rods out without looking like a complete noddy. And you know everyone is looking, even when they're pretending no to. Or am I just being paranoid? Anyway, I would probably have just chucked the rods out anywhere if I was trying to hit the ton plus marks. Wouldn't want everyone to see my rubbish markering and spodding skills. Just been on the IPhone to get the latest on Metcheck. Seems we're in for more wet stuff blowing in on a strong westerly. Looks good for this side of the lake. Anyway, I'm going to start by showing you round my bankside home, welcome to the Bivvy Tramps bivvy tour."

Eighteen

The only place where success comes before work is in the dictionary.

Vidal Sassoon

Things are busy down at Marsh Lakes, with lorries arriving from the continent. This week we've had four carrying clonking great Spanish commons. I helped unload 15 x 20s, nine 30s, five 40s and one 50-pounder, mind blowing stock, worth a fortune. More worryingly, a few white English vans have been turning up with single fish, big mirrors. Fortunately we don't recognise any of them. The last thing Ron, Tommy and I want is a famous fish like the Mother or the Royal Forty turning up at Marsh Lakes. There's no denying it's a fishery full of wrong 'uns and tourists, but somehow the excitement and sheer ambition of the place is infectious. It's Las Vegas-style carp fishing, lots of bells, whistles and bright lights. I'm like Charlie in the chocolate factory. There's something a bit sinister going on, but I can't take my eyes off the amazing carp candy.

One thing is clear, what Harry wants Harry gets. He doesn't respond well to *'no'* or *'can't'*. The toys go straight out of the pram. Watching a grown man having a toddler-style tantrum is hilarious and terrifying, we're all on eggshells around him. He goes scarlet, eyes bulging, forehead sweating and then comes the effing and blinding, arms waving, body twisting in anger and frustration, a full blown Basil Fawlty. Tommy has had a few tricky conversations with him. The worst was when he pointed out that Marsh Lakes is vulnerable to flooding. He went ballistic, saying he doesn't want doubters on his team, and if we don't trust him we can piss off. Slung us all off site, and it took a couple of days for him to calm down and apologise.

The builders have been in overdrive creating our new home in the car park. It could have been a porta-cabin in a muddy car park, but credit to Harry, he's gone the extra mile and then some, with a tiled roof, big windows and splendid raised veranda for the café. I suppose he's got to look at it from his house, so he doesn't want it to look crap. It's gonna be the perfect spot for drinking tea, chatting and keeping an eye on shows in Monsters. If they were allowed, the anglers would be permanently AWOL from their swims with the remotes lined up on the tables. The shop feels palatial compared to Tommy's Tackle. At last we've got a proper showroom, where we can set up bivvies, bedchairs and barrows. This morning we're setting up the two big rod displays and hanging nets, mats and bags from the walls. The bait department boasts four glass-fronted freezers, plenty of space to display all Harry's 'approved' products. So what with commercial rigs and only Marsh-bought baits allowed, he's got the anglers over a barrel. And the list of rules seems to be growing by the day, won't be surprised if he gets one of us going round checking knots. Sorry, going off on one again. A fishery should only need two rules, take absolute care of the fish, and be considerate of other anglers.

"What do you reckon? Not bad is it?" Tommy asks, standing back and admiring his new empire.

"It's pukka mate. What future for Tommy's now?"

"We'll see. The lease is due next January, so if this place really takes off I'll give it up."

"Really, wouldn't feel right not having Tommy's Tackle in St. Ives," I say.

"I know, but like you're always telling me, it's the 21st Century. Maybe it's time to move on."

"Who's going to look after it when we open here?"

"We'll take turns. Harry wants us open seven days a week, so might go down to a five day opening at Tommy's. Let's face it, we're not exactly run off our feet over there are we?"

"I'd be happy to be at Tommy's," I say. "That way I can keep an eye on the Lagoon."

"Ok no problem, novelty of Marsh wearing thin already?"

"Not really I'm sort of enjoying it. But you know my main mission is banking the Lady."

We both lean on the counter, watching the digger tearing up the bank at the back of Monsters Lake.

"It's a mess out there," I say.

"Yeah, but better to have a bit of disruption now, than get flooded out next winter."

"I suppose so. What are they doing today?"

"Well, they've just finished putting a bund round the eastern perimeter, to stop flood water coming in. And now they're digging channels between the lakes, to take the big pipes in the car park," Tommy says.

"Ok, so we can stop water coming in from the flood plain, what about ground water?"

"Good point. I reckon the only way to deal with that is pumping it out over the bund. Look at all the pumps they use in the fens to get water off the farmland and into the drains," Tommy says.

"More expense for Harry though. He will be pleased. Make sure I'm not there when you mention it to him."

"Nah mate, I'll tell him it was your idea. The last bit of pain is building a sluice at the back of the complex. Bund, drains, pumps and sluice should cover most flood situations. The sluice also means we can keep water on site from the spring, so levels don't go down too far in the summer."

"Cool. But will we be ready for the August opening?"

"Sure, they're nearly finished. Those pipes will go in over the next couple of days, and Harry has a load of turf and gravel on order."

"At least we've got a good fence, to keep the fish in and the otters out," I say.

"We could do with one around the St. Ives complex. Bloody otters have been seen out on the islands again."

"You'd have thought there'd be grants to support fisheries," I say.

"I've heard they're giving loads of dosh to projects re-introducing them."

"It doesn't make sense, surely they know fisheries and otters don't mix. There should be money available to both."

"And now we've got endless cormorants to contend with too," Tommy says.

"I know, what's going on at the coast? Seagulls, cormorants, we'll have seals swimming up the Ouse next."

"You're not far off the mark there, they've been seen at Earith a few years back."

"Can't be many fish left in the sea."

"Yeah, that and it's easy pickings for cormorants on our lakes," says Tommy.

"We won't have cormorants at Marsh Lakes."

"Why's that?"

"Ron'll blast 'em to Kingdom come!"

"So what's the news on the Environment Agency visit yesterday?" I ask.

"They were looking at the fencing on the flood plain, It's all fine. A bloke from DEFRA came too. He was checking Harry's importation licences."

"And?"

"According to Harry it was fine. He produced all the required paperwork, and they went away happy. We've got a green light."

"Do you believe it?" I ask.

"Look, I'm in too deep to worry about it now. If they say it's legal, it's legal, end of!"

"You've got to hand it to him, he's got more front than Blackpool."

"I think we could learn a thing or two from Harry," Tommy says.

"What exactly did you have in mind, thieving and smuggling?"

"Bit harsh Kes. Here we are in the nest of the golden goose."

"Treasure Island, more like. I reckon the man's a first rate pirate!"

"Yeah well, keep your gob shut Kes, you know he doesn't take prisoners. You'll be walking the plank with talk like that."

At that moment Harry appears at the window, smiling his gold toothy grin and giving one of his Winston Churchill V signs, cigar in hand.

"Morning lads, how's it going in here?"

"Fantastic," Tommy says.

"Loving the new shop Harry, feels like Harrods," I say, feeling more than a bit two-faced.

"Good one. We've got a Rolls Royce set up all right. And I should know, my wallet is bruised and battered. Still, once we get the drainage sorted we can settle down to business."

"Are we still on for the 1st August opening Harry?" I ask.

"Too bloody right we are. That's why I'm here. This time next week you're all invited to have a crack at Monsters Lake. A bit of R&R before the punters and cash start rolling in."

"Great idea Harry," Tommy says.

"Bring your brollies, weather forecast is atrocious. Heavy rain and gale force winds," Harry says.

"Sounds like perfect fishing weather to me!" I say.

"Maybe, but I've ordered sunshine for opening day. And I won't be best pleased with anything else," Harry says, looking upwards and shaking his fist.

"Have you got God on your side Harry?" I say cheekily.

"Of course Kes, I'll do business with anyone if the price is right," He says.

"Bob Dylan, 1964," Tommy says, winking at me and a puzzled Harry.

Nineteen

We knelt side by side looking at it. I knew it was big, and suddenly it dawned on me it was more than that. It was tremendous! Then we put the fish in a sack and lifted it on my spring balance, which goes up to thirty two pounds. The pointer came up against the stop with such a thump that we both knew at once that here was a new record.

Richard Walker, Stillwater Angling, 1955

t may be high summer but feels like Christmas Eve in the Royal Tavern, the Adnams fuelling our fevered discussions. Ron confesses to having trouble sleeping, waking up in cold sweats having pulled out of a succession of monsters. Tommy admits he's been getting up at 5.00 a.m. for the last week, slipping into Marsh early and baiting a couple of spots. They're not surprised to hear I've got mixed feelings. I'm buzzing about the chance of a new PB, and stressing about being involved at all.

"Hey guys, what do you think, is one of us going to catch some well known lump tomorrow?"

"Give it a rest Kes. Harry has bought a few English fish, but it's all above board," Ron says.

"I hope you're right, but my gut feeling is not good," I say.

"You're off the map again mate! Ain't that right Tommy?"

"I hope so for all our sakes."

"Oh that's bloody nice. Listen to the pair of you. The bloke has single-handedly given us the best fishing in the country on our doorstep, a fantastic business on a plate and we're sitting here slagging him off."

"I'm not slagging him off, just asking a few questions about where the fish came from, and whether filling your garden pond full of whackers and calling it a carp fishery is a good idea," I say.

"Oh stop the world please, Kes wants to get off. Get with the programme mate, it's called progress. This is the modern world!"

"The Jam, 1977," Tommy says.

We all crack up and leave it at that. Conversation returns to tactics for our first session, and all too soon we're heading our separate ways for a bit of much needed shuteye before the big day.

A few restless hours later I sit up in my bunk and peer out on a grey wet fenland morning. High summer, not, that seems to be a thing of the past. Now we have spring, then a couple of weeks of sun at some point between April and September, but otherwise it's wall to wall cloud and rain. It's not too bad for the fishing though. The thermometer hanging outside reads 15 degrees, and my barometer is showing low pressure, perfect fishing weather. I love my iPhone, but you can't beat a bit of old fashioned technology. The kettle goes on for a quick brew to soothe the beer head, and I perch on the stern looking out across the marina. *Ten past five, he's bloody late as usual,* I think and impatiently move my gear outside onto the gravel track. *Where is the lazy swine. I knew it was a mistake to take a lift off Tommy.* Despite my reservations about Marsh, the temptation to haul a Monster is too strong, and the fever is burning away inside me as usual. Not wanting to a waste a minute more, I begin threading boilies onto the rigs. Of course, almost immediately I hear the sound of wheels crunching on the gravel. "You won't catch anything there mate! Get your gear in, you're gonna make me late," Tommy says, not missing the opportunity for a wind-up even at five, no let's be precise, five sixteen in the morning.

Tommy puts his foot down and we speed our way from the Boathaven up Low Road to Fenstanton. "Well, should be a cracking day Kes! Hope you've got some good line on those reels?"

"Oh yes, don't worry about me. I'm loaded up with brand new 17lb X-line. Checked all knots, and my hooks are sticky sharp. Anything that comes anywhere near these rigs will be nailed. I'm in the zone this morning. Just watch me go!"

"You know who would have loved this," Tommy says.

I don't say anything. We both know Dad would have been as high as a kite, fishing for monsters like we've got in Marsh.

"He's with us in spirit Kes, that's for sure."

Soon we're heading down onto the flood plain at the back of the village, Marsh Lakes on our left. The smell of coffee and bacon wafts invitingly across the Marsh Lodge car park. Inside, Ron is busy in the kitchen.

"Morning chaps. Thought you'd changed your minds," beams Harry, sitting at a table flicking through his stock book.

"Choosing which fish you're going to catch first Harry?" I ask, resisting the temptation to have a dig at Tommy.

"Just whetting my appetite Kes."

Ron brings in a plate of doorstep sarnies, and we discuss who'll fish where. Ron fancies the islands swim round the back. Tommy chooses the point, and I opt for the bay. Harry has already set up on his lawn, full of confidence.

"I've kept baits going in every couple of days, so you guys just sit back and enjoy the show. I'll be hauling all day." I'm not convinced Harry's much of an angler, but don't' say anything, after all it is his lake. He's certainly got the right gear, but has he got any idea?

I'm first to cast, placing a bait on a small mound in the deepest part of the bay, and one either end of the island. Twenty freebies are fired around each and I settle back into dad's old comfy day chair. Round the lake traps are set, everything is still and silent, each in our own private theatre of carpy dreams. An hour passes, huddled under my new, second hand from Tommy, JRC Stealth brolly, watching the water dripping onto my boots, and scanning the lake for any sign of hope. Then, *HURRAH!* off the point of the island in front of me a huge fish pushes its head and shoulders out of the water. "*Hello to you too!*" I think and edge closer to my rods. "*I'm on the fish, and they're moving.*"

A buzzer screams into life, I jump up, confused, nothing seems to be moving. "Happy days" comes a shout from across the lake, I look round to see Tommy, not Harry, bent into a fish.

"I thought I was the one going deaf Tommy. Turn your alarms down will ya!" I shout.

"Just sharing the sweet sound of success," Tommy says, the swine.

"Good Man," shouts Harry, punching the air and whipping out his bins for a closer look. Credit to Harry, he does look genuinely pleased to see a fish on someone else's hook.

Tommy expertly coaxes the fish into open water and quickly has it on a short line. A few short lunges later, and he draws the landing net up around the first ever Marsh Lakes' capture.

"How big?" Ron shouts across the lake.

Tommy laughs, "It's one of the small ones, a common, only about 35lb."

"*What a place,*" I think.

The next few hours pass without incident. "Lunch time," Harry calls out.

The lovely Georgia has laid out a fabulous spread in the Lodge, roast beef sandwiches, washed down with bottles of London Pride, and apple pie and cream for pudding. Pukka Tucker!

"Had a nice morning boys?"

"Great lunch Mrs P," I say.

"You can call me Georgia love."

"Georgia Love, what a nice name" I say.

"Oi cheeky," says Georgia giggling and tottering off in her high heels.

"Chatting up my wife now are we? I can see I'm going to have to keep my eye on you," says Harry.

"Sorry Harry, just having a laugh."

"Yeah, very funny I'm sure," Harry says taking a long sup on his beer bottle, but not taking his eyes off me.

Whoops! Better be more careful about flirting with Georgia.

"So, looks like I'm top rod then," Tommy says, thankfully rescuing me, again.

"That's probably one of the Spanish fish," Harry says, "from a well-known river full of cats."

The reality of this fishing heaven surfaces but no one says anything.

"Don't worry boys, it's all fine and dandy. Got special permission to move a few."

"I saw a big fish roll in my swim, must have been pushing 50lb," I say.

We forget our doubts. The spell is working again, and tactics are discussed over a second round of beers.

"Right lads let's get back out there and catch another whacker," Harry says.

I decide to try something different, putting Snowman rigs with four-bait stringers on each rod, and scaling down to size tens. Harry is shaping up for a cast to the island as I bend down to adjust my bobbins. Glancing back up I see his rod bent double. *Bloody hell, that was quick*, I think. *Must have dropped right on its head.* The fish powers round the tip of the island. He hangs on, his line shaking the overhanging branches. Suddenly a loud crack echoes across the lake. "Arse burgers," shouts Harry, throwing his rod javelin style up the lawn, as he stamps off towards the house. Whoops, not good! I pull my hood up and zip my jacket against the north wind blowing in, mean and unseasonal on this surreal summer day. *What should I do?* There's been action at either end of the lake, so the fish are obviously well spread. Still got the whole afternoon and evening, *plenty of time*, I reassure myself. *You've got good baits in good spots. Everything is set up nicely, just be patient!* It's that same old dilemma, do I try to make something happen or will that just bugger up my swim? If in doubt have a brew! I decide to leave everything. On goes the iPod, time for a bit of mid-session psychotherapy from Mr Manson.

The hours slip by without further incident. Harry is back in his swim swigging bottles of London Pride, but hasn't said a word, or bothered to pick up the rod on the lawn. We have to pack up at nine, so less than ten minutes to rescue a first blank on Marsh. Not for Tommy though, he's already had his prize, and is wheeling his barrow round. What can I do to buy a bite? I try a few take-inducing rituals like breaking down my landing net, turning off my buzzers, and walking across the track for a piss. No Good. I wind in my left-hand rod and stow it away.

"See you all tomorrow," Harry shouts, shuffling away dejectedly.

Tommy appears behind me. "Poor old Harry, he's like a kid who's broken his new toy on his birthday."

"Oh well, he'll have his day. Lucky he didn't have a run while he was off sulking, else he'd have lost a second fish round the back of the island," I say.

"True. Ron is disgusted, you know he hates people leaving their swim with their rods in. It's a hanging offence in Ron's world."

"So what's the trick then? I'm struggling here."

"Nothing special, I just figured they'd be suckers for a Snowman with a pink fluoro pop-up. Hard to reel in isn't it!" Tommy says.

"I was sure I was going to catch," I say, "reckon Harry lost that fish I saw."

"Maybe, but you'll have plenty of chances over the next few months."

"I don't think so. I'll be working when I'm here, and then fishing over the Lagoon or in Tommy's. I just assumed we'd be hauling all day long."

"Ah well, that's carp fishing for you. Don't forget these fish haven't really had much time to settle down, and they're not stock fish used to eating pellets all day long."

"True, I suppose I just wanted to get one and then move on. I'm sort of enjoying it, and sort of not."

"Typical of you Kes, overanalysing everything, just chill out, it's only a day's fishing."

As the boilie on the middle rod comes skimming across the surface, my right-hand rod jumps in the pod, the tip bends round and line rips from the reel.

I throw the middle rod at Tommy, click the Baitrunner off and pull into a fish. Jumping straight into the water I wade to my right, keeping the rod up high. "Shit, that's colder than I thought!"

"Don't worry about that, you could have a British record on the other end."

"Oh no pressure then," I laugh. "Don't think wrong 'uns count!"

"Concentrate Kes this is no time for one of your rants. Where's your net?"

"I packed it away," I say sheepishly.

"You wally!"

"Yeah, but it worked didn't it."

"You and your Harry Potter magic tactics. I think we'll call you Dumbledore from now on."

Tommy sets up the net, while I hang onto a super angry fish, steaming along the front of Harry's Island. It surfaces under the trees, shaking its head, sending nerve shattering vibrations down the line. For what feels like minutes, but can only be seconds, we're locked in a stalemate, both knowing that this is where the battle will be won and lost. If the fish gets round the island, it will win. I can feel the rod butt bending as I give her all I've got.

"It's like a bloody hippo on the other end, I can't move it."

"Don't panic. Keep the pressure on. The next move is hers!"

And then suddenly she gives, moving out into deeper water, away from immediate danger.

Tommy grabs the waders off his barrow, wrestles for all he's worth into the neoprene and joins me in the water. I need all the help I can get.

"Feels bloody big," I say.

"What did you get it on?"

I laugh, "Snowman with a pink fluoro pop-up!"

"Good work Kes, you know it makes sense!"

A huge grey shape swims past, deep down just off the marginal shelf. We look each other, eyes wide, jaws open.

"Holy shit!" I say.

"I think you hooked a passing submarine."

"Please don't fall off."

"What Size hook have you got on?

"Size ten?"

"Bloody hell, you're a braver man than me!"

"These JRC hooks are the dogs, built for monsters!" I say confidently, feeling anything but.

"Let's not think about it falling off. Should be alright, just keep her coming, nice and easy. Let her tire herself out, no big dangers nearby."

The line jerks, the water boils and I forget to breathe. Up and down she goes, using the deep water and her weight to test my tackle. Crikey my arm, it's bloody agony. I nestle the butt of the rod in my crotch, and use my left arm to hold it just below the first eye. Somehow she senses another chance and flat rods me, ripping line off the clutch. Thankfully, for once, I have it set properly. That was her swan song as for the first time she surfaces in front of us. A giant mouth emerges from the water with my very small hook in the middle of the bottom lip. Nailed. A few more lunges and she's beaten, wallowing on the surface gulping air. Tommy takes a step forward, pushing out with the net and scoops her up in one go. "Monster!"

For the next couple of minutes I do my usual headless chicken act, running around grabbing camera, scales, water, looking for the best spot to do the pictures. "Calm down Kes."

"You're right. Sorry."

"Don't apologise, enjoy. It's a special moment."

"It feels pretty good, surreal but good."

"Excellent, so no more talking, just go and get your weighsling, I don't trust this net," Tommy says.

Together we haul the fish onto the mat. Ron appears behind us, " my god, what a beauty!" We all stare in silence, awestruck by the huge chestnut flank scattered with characteristic apple slice scales

"We know this fish don't we, well over 60lb," Ron whispers.

"Could be 70!" Tommy says earnestly. "Looks like the one we saw Istvan put in."

"Come on, let's find out," I say.

Ron zeros in the scales, then Tommy and I lift her into my new, second hand from the boot sale, Trakker weighsling. Off the floor she comes, and we watch as the needle spins round, 20...30...40....50...60....67....69lb.

"69lb 12oz," Ron says looking at me. "You know what you've bloody gone and done don't you?"

"What?" I say.

"You've broken the British record!" Tommy says.

"Oh my god, but it doesn't count does it?" I say.

"Probably not, but it's still the biggest carp ever caught in England," Ron says.

We put her back in the water, while Tommy rings Harry. "You'd better get down here, Kes has caught something a bit special."

He comes charging down the lawn waving a bottle of champagne above his head, apparently over earlier disappointments, or just buoyed by the umpteenth London Pride.

"How big?" he shouts. None of us says anything, "come on, how big, get her on the mat."

"Wow, it's one of the big Hungarian mirrors," he says. "She was just over 70lb when she went in. Kes you've put us on the map, a new record, the first ever UK 70-pounder."

"Not quite, 69lb 12oz," I say.

"Bad luck!" Harry says.

Ron and Tommy find this hilarious. It takes Harry a second to catch on. We all have a good laugh, exhilarated by the fantasy carping at Marsh Lakes.

"Not a bad little fishery I've got here is it chaps?"

"Not too shabby," Tommy says holding a net full of mirror in the water.

"I hope you're feeling strong. She's going to take some lifting." Ron says.

I feel pretty nervous dealing with such a massive beast, especially as Harry is fussing around me about every little detail. It's not surprising, after all, he probably paid a lot of money for her.

"Lift her head up a bit," Tommy says, "and smile, you're supposed to look happy."

"I can't smile it's too heavy."

"Just grimace for the camera then!"

Twenty

Many go fishing all their lives without knowing that it is not fish they are after.

Henry David Thoreau

Yesterday I was thrilled with the Marsh Lakes' monster. It was a lovely fish, in many ways the fish of a lifetime. And of course we celebrated in style. Champagne at Harry's, followed by beer at the Floods Tavern and then the obligatory curry blowout at the Sultan on London Road. But sitting here on *Kingfisher* this morning, staring out across the river towards the Lagoon, doubts are swirling round my mind. *It's not really a British record. A few months ago it was swimming around in Hungary. It's not real. It doesn't count.* Harry hasn't helped, he was straight on to Carp-Talk and Angling Times bigging it up, making all sorts of claims. Apparently they're both running stories and pictures of the fish. It's caused a bit of a stir and not a little controversy. Angling Times are coming up next week to do a feature on Marsh Lakes. Tommy and Harry are chuffed to bits with all the attention, and worse, they want me there for more shots and interviews. Great, just what I wanted, NOT! *X-treme Carping*? Fishing for tourists in Harry's garden pond, I don't think so.

I feel the need for a reality check so dig out my old spinning rod and head off along the river towards the Hemingfords. Still raining, in fact it's been hammering down non-stop for 48 hours, and the river is starting to swell. The summer boating brigade, moored on the meadow, are all huddled in their cabins, drinking tea and staring anxiously at the sky. Probably wondering if they'll get back safely to their moorings. I find a bit of slack water just below Hemingford lock and flick out a small lure alongside some rushes on the near bank. Almost immediately the rod tip jerks round and an aggressive little jack wrestles and shakes his head. It jumps clear of the water, tail walking impressively. I quickly draw it into shallow water and put my small net under it. The fenland tiger lays there on the wet grass, staring. "Pike, three inches long, perfect, pike in all parts, green tigering the gold, killers from the egg," that's Ted Hughes mate, he wrote a poem about you lot.

Somehow that little pike has earthed all the stress buzzing around inside me. This is what it's all about, me, the river, the weather and a wild animal. Perfect indeed! This is what I want from my carp fishing too. I feel a whole lot better about the circus surrounding Marsh Lakes and the 'record fish'. It means nothing, just carp fishing business, not real carp fishing. Not to me anyway. I flick out the treble hook with my forceps, put the little fella back in the water and watch him scuttle off at top speed.

"Morning Kes!" The smiling face of Jay greets me as I turn.

"Surprised to see you on the river at this time of year, giving the Lagoon carp a rest?"

"Yeah, just fancied a walk in the rain," I say.

"Want a cuppa? We're moored just upstream."

I'm a bit surprised by the invite, as I was under the impression I'm the enemy.

"Not going to take me hostage are you?" I joke.

"Ah well maybe, but you know Saira doesn't usually take prisoners, she's straight in for the kill."

"Yeah, I've always thought she was extremely aggressive for a pacifist."

"She's tough on the outside, but has a heart of gold you know!" Jay says.

"Neil Young, 1972."

"Sorry?"

"Don't mind me. Whenever I hear a lyric I have to blurt out the artist and year of release."

"You've always been a music anorak haven't you? I remember at school, you started that pop quiz club."

"Oh yeah, don't remind me, that was very sad."

We laugh and head up above the lock. This should be interesting, Saira in her own environment.

The *Heron* is Jay's old narrowboat. I have to say I like the battered lived in look, its flaking green paint patched up with splotches of black, and the roof a jumble of bikes, wood, ropes, and blue tarpaulin. Dad would have disapproved. Everything on *Kingfisher* was ship shape and Bristol fashion when he was skipper. Saira and Jay have been living afloat for a couple of years, cruising between St. Ives and Huntingdon. I'm curious, as I've never been invited in before. But I suppose it's something we actually do have in common, and you're supposed to be friendly on the river. The cabin is warm and cosy, joss stick smouldering by the window filling the air with hippy fragrance. Saira is reading, nestled in a large beanbag in front of a small wood burning stove. She looks distinctly unimpressed to see me entering her world.

"Look who I found skulking around outside."

Saira grunts and returns to her book.

"Don't mind her, she's always a grumpy sod in the mornings."

Despite the less than enthusiastic welcome, The Raconteurs are sending good vibrations through the bulkheads, and we discuss the merits of Jack White's song writing, neutral territory for us both. It doesn't last long though, as Jay goes fishing himself.

"I hear a new fishery is opening in Fenstanton?"

"Yeah, that's right."

"What do you think about it?"

"What do you mean? It's going to be very popular, lots of big fish."

"Yeah, but what do you think about sticking loads of fish in a hole in the ground?" Jay asks.

"They're not holes in the ground, quite nice lakes actually."

"It's not natural though is it?"

"No it's not, and there are plenty of carp anglers who don't agree with it either."

"It's outrageous," Saira says, without looking up from her book, but clearly armed and ready.

"There's no law against it," I say.

"Not yet!" She says.

"Who is this Harry Plant?" Jay asks.

"Well, I don't know much about him really, except that he runs a waste management business and now has a carp fishery in his back garden."

"Where did the fish come from?"

"Bloody hell, am I being interrogated here?"

"Well kind of. I'll give you a biscuit," Jay says, laughing.

"So about these fish, are they English?"

"Some, but mostly imported from Europe?"

"Is that legal?"

"Apparently, DEFRA have been down and checked all his paperwork."

"It's disgusting, bringing those fish halfway across Europe," Saira says, launching a first missile.

"I agree, you shouldn't be able to bring big fish into England. And despite what you think I am concerned with animal welfare."

"That's such bullshit Kes, you spend all your spare time trying to stick hooks in fish. That's not a concern with animal welfare!"

"Here we go again. What I'm talking about is avoiding wiping out whole stocks of fish by introducing diseases like KHV, carp herpes."

"And the hooks don't damage their mouths?"

"It can happen, I accept, but we feed them like kings and queens, look after their homes and treat them with great care when we do catch them. It's not such a bad life."

"Come on Saira, give it a rest. I didn't invite Kes in for you to give him another verbal bashing."

"Yeah Saira, you can save that for the demos down the river. Anyway, I thought you only did the *FishAction* bit when you had your bikini on," I say grinning.

"You're not funny you know, and I'll never accept it," she says, and returns to her book.

"I think we'll have to do a bit of investigating, see what we can find out about Harry Plant?"

"I'd be careful if I were you. He's well connected and has a very short fuse," I say.

"Oh don't worry about that, I'm well connected too and very good at digging for dirt."

Fortunately Jay seems as keen as me to get off the subject, and we talk for a while about our musical aspirations, and the much safer subject of guitars. He shows me his very cool Guild acoustic, and I can't resist the opportunity to run through my repertoire of licks. Even Saira stops reading, not smiling, but not scowling either.

"Show off!" She says.

"Don't listen to her. What was that last chord sequence? Sounded amazing."

While I'm showing Jay a few of my secrets on the fret board, a thought pops into my mind.

"I know what you guys are. You're just the latest in a long line of Huntingdonshire radicals. You're following in Oliver Cromwell's footsteps, shaking up the status quo."

"What do you reckon we are then, Ranters, Diggers or Levellers?" Jay asks.

"Oh Saira is definitely a Ranter. An anarchist in a black bikini! How 21st Century!" I say, conscious that I seem unable to refer to Saira without mentioning her bikini.

"You've got her number, definitely a Ranter!"

"Piss off you two! What's a Ranter?"

"Someone who rants like you," I say.

"Yeah yeah, and...?"

"They were a group... who... er... hang on, I'll look them up on Wikipedia," I say reaching inside my jacket for my iPhone.

"Tasty bits of kit, aren't they! Jay says.

"Definitely. The future's bright, the future's, err...Apple!" I say.

"Have you got a book of daft comments, or do you really spend your life making them up?"

"Ouch, you heard what Jay said, best behaviour for your guests. Here we are... the Ranters, a radical English sect in the time of the Commonwealth, 1649 to 1660, their central idea was pantheistic, that God is essentially in every creature. Well that's you lot for sure. They were obviously the original Bunnyhuggers!"

"Actually that's pretty cool. I've decided, I am a 21st century Ranter," Saira says.

"I'll design you a Ranters' T-shirt!" I say.

"Quite a good name for a band," Jay says.

"What else does it say?" Saira asks.

"Well loads of blah blah about religion, but this is definitely you Saira," I say, laughing.

"What?"

"Ranters were regarded as a threat to social order. Yes, you, and were often associated with nudity. Definitely you, always stripping down to that black bikini, I rest my case."

"You're making that up," Saira shrieks.

"I'm not, look. Nudity was used as a social protest and a symbol of abandoning earthly goods. Ranters were accused of fanaticism, sexual immorality and locked up in prison until they recanted."

"Good for them. Sounds like they were radical free thinkers," Jay says.

"Plenty of time for thinking in jail," I say.

"Your point being?"

"Err....you break the law, you end up in jail!"

"Sometimes it's worth it," Jay says.

"And sometimes it's not," I say.

We both know where this is heading, but I decide to bail out before Saira's hackles are raised again. "Well guys. Thanks for the coffee. I think I'd better make tracks. Keep on ranting Saira!"

"I will. Sell your fishing gear on *ebay* while you've got the chance."

"I thought it was me who specialised in daft comments," I say.

"And the ref blows his whistle. It's one all, at the end of the game. I'll see you out Kes, before we get into extra time and penalties."

The rain is still falling as we emerge onto the stern of the *Heron*.

"Bit grim for August!" I say.

"Certainly is. So when will this Marsh Lakes place open?"

"Next week. Why, going to run a feature on it in the sports section of the paper?" I ask.

"I won't be pitching it to the editor, put it that way."

"I thought it was exactly the kind of thing the Town Crier loves."

"Sadly Kes, you're right, which is why I'm getting out of there as soon as I can. Anyway, the editor isn't too impressed about my involvement with *FishAction*."

"I'm not surprised, slight conflict of interests there."

"Only if I write about it. Not the sort of thing I can generally include in the Entertainment section. The Huntingdon players are doing a version of Midsummer Night's Dream, Brotherhood of Man are playing the Commemoration Hall, Radiation are at the Royal Tavern, AGAIN, and by the way I think fishing is cruel, let's ban it!"

"Very funny, but you can still influence the editor."

"Have you met him? His favourite saying is 'When I want your opinion, I'll give it to you!'"

"Anyway, just stay away from Marsh Lakes, Harry Plant doesn't take prisoners."

"Thanks for the advice."

The rain is really hammering down now, I pick up my rod and net and wander back towards the thicket, taking the occasional cast in between the trees hoping to tempt something a bit bigger. I've heard rumours of big perch in this stretch, should have a go for one this winter. I pause in the churchyard, sitting on the wall, chucking the spinner absent-mindedly downstream. The rain drips off the peak of dad's old army waterproof. He would have loved watching me catch that big mirror. I can just imagine him, stressing about how I was handling it, taking ages to get the right angle for the perfect shot. I pull out my wallet and have a quick look at the picture of him with Paddle from the Woolpack, his PB. *Miss you dad!* The rain seems to have even put the jacks off the feed, so I head past the museum and into town for an all-day breakfast at Joe's café, the perfect antidote to any hangover.

Your success in carp fishing is measured by the pleasure you derive from it.

Tim Paisley, Carp Fishing, 1988

'm on a roll, first fish from the Lagoon, the Marsh Lakes monster, and this morning another awesome haul at the boot sale. I found a chap selling 400 carp magazines. Stacks of them, *Carpworld, Carp Fisher, Big Carp, Advanced Carp Fishing,* and *Carpology.* Back copies of these can sell at their original cover price, so there I was drooling over maybe a grand's worth of booty, trying to pick the right moment to make my move. Fortunately he blew his cover first. "A hundred quid for the lot." It's a steal, but can I be bothered selling individual copies to fussy collectors on *ebay* and hundreds of trips to the Post Office? I got on the blower to Tommy and convinced him we could make a profit selling them in the shop. He nipped down and we took the lot. The other bonus being we're now stocked up on pukka reading material between customers.

Chillaxing on *Kingfisher* to the sound of Slayer (it does it for me), the chemical wonders of Adnams ale and 20 boot sale mags, aka, *carp porn*! In my grubby paws is Advanced Carp Fishing from August 2003. The cover picture shows that unstoppable carp fishing force Jim Shelley with the great Two-Tone from Conningbrook at 61lbs 4oz. Second session on and he's bagged the biggest carp in the country. Awesome angling or luck? I'm going with the former, cos he's done it time again wherever he's fishing, taking waters apart. I'm pretty fickle and jump around from one mag to another, depending on who's featured. I'll buy anything with Terry Hearn or Peter Springate on the cover. Another favourite is Leon Bartropp. The man knows his rigs! But when it comes to sheer entertainment you have to go a long way to beat Pete Regan, carp fishing's filthy minded raconteur par excellence.

The magazine I grew up with was Carpworld. Dad bought it every month. As a kid I'd read it in bed, late into the night, nestled under the covers with a torch, marvelling at the seemingly impossible feats of my heroes. All the best anglers have written for Carpworld at some point, it's like a who's who of carping royalty. Check out some of these Carpworld cover stars from the nineties to the noughties: Lee Jackson December 1991, Kevin Nash September 1996, Kevin Maddocks February 1997, Peter Springate September 2001, Dave Lane August 2002, Frank Warwick September 2002, Alijn Danau July 2003, Steve Briggs September 2003, Rob Farrant November 2008, Terry Hearn August 2010. Top drawer or what! And if you thought *Fitty of the month* was a recent innovation, check out the babes in the Fishabil adverts on the back of the 2002 Carpworlds. I'm feeling hot hot hot!

Staring at the gargantuan and elusive Two-Tone has given me the next game for the shop, bound to cause endless argument, top five UK carp captures of all time. Nice! I need to get my list sorted. Back in 1952, the record was Bob Richard's 31lb 4oz Redmire mirror, until Richard Walker smashed it with Clarissa at 44lb. So that's the obvious choice for top spot. It was like catching a UK 70-pounder today, and most people at the time were struggling to catch their first double. But, and I know this is practically heretical, does it look 44lb to you? Anyway, I'd better leave it there. Let's just accept that they did a proper job on the weighing. At least they didn't knock it on the head, even if it did spend the rest of its life swimming in circles at London Zoo. You could make a case for the first recorded non-Redmire 40, Ray Clay's 42lb common from Billing Aquadrome in 1966. Pretty special!

While we're on the subject of Redmire, most people would put the first UK fifty pounder on the list, Chris Yates and "The Bishop" at 51lb 6oz. I'm not so sure it's in my top five though. It's my Redmire prejudice coming out again, too small, and too exclusive back then. Tommy and Ron will string me up by the wotsits if it's not on the list. Don't get me wrong, I'm a massive fan of Chris Yates and his 'brothers of the angle' approach, split cane, freelined sweetcorn and all that, but I'm going to big-up carp caught from *X-treme* waters. Everyone has a soft spot for the late great Bazil from Yately North Lake, and as a kid I remember marvelling at pictures of Ritchie Macdonald with it at 45lb 12oz in 1984. What about the first UK 60-pounder? I think I'm right in saying that this was Gary Bayes and his capture of Two-Tone from Conningbrook in 2001, at the truly monster weight of 61lb.

Another capture that has always stood out in my mind as being truly phenomenal is the Yeoveney brace of upper 30s taken by Peter Springate in 1978. The photos on the back cover of *Carp Fever* fired my imagination as a kid. In my opinion, it is still up there as a piece of pioneering fishing for unknown whackers, something the great man repeated in his exploits at Wraysbury. Some of you probably think his brace of Mary and Mary's Mate should be on there, and it's a good call. If anyone deserves to be on that list then it's Sir

Peter Springate. I'm going for Walker at number one, Springate at two, and for bringing Mary ashore at a new record weight of 55lb 13oz from the ultra difficult Wraysbury I've got Terry Hearn at number three. For similar reasons I'm putting Nigel Sharp on the list. I mean five years and two bikes later (fish spotting on 100 acres is not for wimps) he banks the most amazing fish in England, the Burghfield common at 52lb 12oz, only her fourth capture as a whacker.

My top five UK carp captures of all time are:

Dick Walker — 44lb common, Redmire, 1952

Peter Springate — 38lb 8oz & 36lb 8oz mirrors, Yeoveney, 1978

Terry Hearn — Mary at 55lb 13oz, Wraysbury, 1996

Nigel Sharp — The Burghfield Common, 52lb 12oz, 2006

Gary Bayes — Two-Tone, 61lb 2oz, Conningbrook, 2001

Bound to cause days of heated discussion. I think the punters in Tommy's Tackle will approve, even if Ron and Tommy don't. I close my eyes and drift off with carp swimming around my brain:

Welcome to Radio Gaga, live from a chilly Abbey Stadium in Cambridge. Today sees the inaugural match between Advanced Carp Fishing United and the Carpworld Allstars. It's not a pretty sight, a motley assortment of shapes and sizes in severely strained nylon. But what some lack in physical prowess, is compensated by their cunning, guile, and grim determination. And we're off. Hearn slips the ball to Crow, who spotting Stewart taking an early drink from his flask, attempts an audacious 50-yard shot, a la Beckham. ACF United scream as one at their aberrant goalie, who turns just in time to take it full in the face. What a save! Stewart still rubbing his hooter rolls the ball out to Clarke on the left, who slips it past Ford to the eager Chillcott. A lovely Van Basten step over from Chillcott, and he's past the Carpworld right back Farrant. He puts in a delicate floated cross to the back stick. Peck nods it down to the waiting Bartropp, who strikes without hesitation and it's in the onion bag. One nil to ACF United!

It's a different Carpworld who've emerged after the break. Their captain Paisley has done a good job in the changing room. Crow and Forward are really starting to dominate the midfield. And here comes Farrant on the overlap down the right. He tries to slip it past Clarke, but it's out for their first corner of the match. Hutchinson comes over to take it, and the two Carpworld centre backs Fairbrass and Kavanagh have their first chance to join the attack. Fairbrass flicks the ball at the near post, and Stewart makes a sharp one handed save. Crow is the first to react. Back to goal, he throws up his left leg, ball dropping over his left shoulder. He is still rising as his right leg comes through. A perfect over head kick, and the ball rifles in off the cross bar. One all! And that's it, the ref blows his whistle, honours even at the end of the match!

	Advanced CarpFishing Utd	CarpworldAllstars
Goal keeper	Richard Stewart	Tim Paisley
Left back	Damian Clarke	Keith Jones
Right back	Dave Moore	Rob Farrant
Centre back	Jim Shelley	Danny Fairbrass
Centre back	Simon Scott	Mike Kavanagh
Left midfield	Nick Helleur	Jake Langley-Hobbs
Right midfield	Tom Dove	Martin Ford
Centre midfield	Ian Chillcott	Paul Forward
Centre midfield	Steve Renyard	Simon Crow
Striker	Darrell Peck	Terry Hearn
Striker	Leon Bartropp	Rod Hutchinson

Twenty-Two

The two best times to fish is when it's rainin' and when it ain't.

Patrick F. McManus

ars are lined up all the way down the lane, bunting flapping wildly in the gale force southwesterly, rain splatting the windscreen. Every few yards anglers are chatting eagerly and earnestly, brimful of pre-session excitement and confidence. Harry taps his watch and scowls as I pull into the car park, but fortunately a camera crew distracts his attention. Hanging from the shop, a large banner welcomes you to, *Marsh Lakes - Where dreams come true!* In front of the steps, a table draped with army netting holds three camo buckets, one for the swim draw on each lake. Tommy is in the shop, preparing prizes, first fish and biggest fish of the day on each lake, and a variety of cash prizes for the tagged fish on the prize fishing lake. Roll up for casino carping!

"Morning Tommy, sorry I'm late."

"No worries, what's it like out there?"

"Busy, wet and blowing a bloody hoolie. Are we still on for a 7.00 a.m. draw?"

"Yeah should be, just waiting for Harry to finish with the TV and the press. Have you seen who's pitched up for the Town Crier?"

"Jay?"

"Oh yes, self-appointed spokesman for the fishes."

"I thought he only covered bands and plays and stuff like that," I say.

"Well he's got himself in, don't know if it's official or not."

"Should I have a word with him?" I ask.

"Don't worry, I've got Ron on him. You take this list of booked anglers and check them off as they come in."

"What's Harry going to be doing?"

"Hosting, which roughly translated, means poking his nose into everything and generally being a pain in the arse."

"No change there then, should be a fun day though!"

All swims are booked, five anglers on Monsters Lake, ten on Willow, and 20 for the prize fishing. Tickets cost £40 on Monsters, £30 on Willow, and £25 on the prize fishing lake, which by my calculation, means Harry will take in a grand in the first 24 hours. Of course, he's giving out a stack of prize money today, but looks like Marsh Lakes is a cash cow, or is that a cash carp? Tommy reckons he'll sell at least two kilos of bait to each angler, and of course they have to buy ready-made rigs from the shop. So that's at least five hundred notes on bait, and maybe £250 on rigs, not to mention other bits and bobs, and there's grub sales too. Could easily be another grand a day in the shop, and probably a couple of hundred from the café. Not sure exactly what deal Tommy's done with Harry, but must be a good time for us to ask for a bigger wedge. Our £50 a day suddenly seems a bit undervalued! Brothers of the angle, aka Ron and Kes, time for us to unite and exercise our collective bargaining power, which actually means, plucking up courage for a quiet word down the pub once Tommy's had a few beers.

Everyone is gathering round the draw table when it kicks off. You guessed it, Saira, Jane, Danny and the rest of *FishAction* appear at the gates waving banners and shouting their well-rehearsed slogans. The camera crew is straight onto them. Seems like this was the story they were really after.

"Ok, can we just ignore those idiots, and get on with our opening draw," says Harry, doing his best to remain upbeat and calm.

Jay, the dodgy double agent, is leading the journalists in gathering quotes from *FishAction*. It only takes a few minutes before Harry's patience cracks. He stomps over to the gates, throws them open, and stands eyeball to eyeball with Saira.

"I think it would be best if you decide to leave!"

"We're not going anywhere, and you can't do a thing about it," Saira hisses, looking every bit as menacing.

Harry ignores this comment and stares up at the grey sky for a couple of seconds, rain dripping off the end of his nose. I'm almost expecting him to throw a wobbly, but fortunately he conquers that instinct and instead turns towards the journalists.

"Everyone who wants to cover the fishing can you please go over by the shop. The rest of you can piss off!"

The hacks shuffle around, not sure where to position themselves for the best story. In the confusion Saira and Jane seize their chance. They drop their banners and make a run for it, straight towards Monsters Lake.

To my surprise, I'm not usually the heroic sort, I shout "Oh no you don't" and launch myself at Jane, grabbing hold of her dungarees. She hits the ground hard, head smashing into the gravel, blood trickling from her eyebrow piercing.

"Sorry Jane," I say, "you're not allowed in here."

"Let me go!" she shrieks, wriggling, kicking and punching for all she's worth.

"Good lad Kes," Harry says, charging past me after Saira.

Ron comes to my aid and puts her in an arm lock. "You're trespassing my dear."

"Get off me, you bloody big oaf!"

Saira quickly strips down to you know what, and wades knee deep in Monsters.

"If you swim in my lake, you'll bloody regret it," Harry shouts.

"Oh yeah, I don't think so. Nice of you to make us a nice new swimming pond Mr Plant, shame about the weather" and out she goes to the sound of press cameras firing.

Some wag shouts "Can you drop a few boilies off the island while you're out there love", followed by, "and I'll dry you off in my bivvy when you come out." Laughter all round, but another voice pipes up, "bitch has ruined the fishing!"

Tommy pulls me aside, "see what you can do Kes, she might listen to you."

"Me? What makes you think that? I'll try, but you can see what she's like."

Saira waves for the cameras, in between shouting, "No more blood sports!"

I wander down to the lake, just along from where the anglers and journalists are gathered. Saira is treading water halfway out to the island.

"Come on Saira, you've made your point," I urge.

"Sod off Kes, I'll come out when I'm ready."

"These guys have all paid good money to fish here today."

"Well Mr Plant can give it back to them, can't he!"

Tommy and Harry are standing on the edge of the car park, wondering exactly what they've done to deserve this amount of grief on their big day.

"She's not coming out," I say.

"Do you think I can shoot trespassers?" Harry asks.

"Tempting, but I wouldn't recommend it with a TV crew on your shoulder," Tommy says.

"How about getting the police down?" I ask.

"No thanks, that really would piss on my parade, a load of coppers poking their noses in. This is bloody doing my head in," Harry says as he stomps down to the lake to exchange a few more pleasantries with Saira. Ron is still sitting on Jane, who seems to have accepted she's bitten off more than she can chew with the Marsh Lakes bailiff. He looks over at us with a, *what do I do now look?* Tommy and I go over to give him a hand.

"You know they've been filming me?" Ron says.

"This is your 15 minutes of fame," I say.

"Not what I would have chosen. Are the police coming?"

"No, Harry doesn't want them down here," Tommy says.

"Whoops, don't think anyone told the press," I say, to the sound of a police siren growing louder in the distance.

"The nice policemen are going to take you away," Ron says.

Jane doesn't say anything, just struggles a bit more and snarls. She certainly looks fearsome with her crew cut, face piercings, and star tattoo on the back of her neck.

"You've got a live one there," Tommy says.

"That's for sure, she keeps trying to bite me."

"I thought she'd be vegetarian," Tommy says, laughing.

Apparently Jane isn't in the mood for jokes, because she just turns her head and spits in my direction.

"Charming!" Ron says.

It's now 10.00 a.m., bivvies and brollies are up, *FishAction*, police and press have gone.

"Well done Kes, I think Harry would have blown a gasket if it had gone on much longer," Tommy says.

"Nothing I did, she just decided to come out, they'd got what they wanted by that point, plenty of attention from the TV and press."

"Well, you helped to keep a lid on it."

"She's got some spirit hasn't she?" I say.

"She must cause that Jay a lot of grief, the way she goes on."

"Oh they're as nutty as each other, totally committed."

"You mean should be committed, to the loony bin," Tommy says.

"One thing's for sure, they've put Harry in a total rage."

"I just hope someone catches a fish now. It might calm him down a bit."

"There are some very wet and grumpy blokes out there. I tell you what Kes, you go round and take tea and coffee orders. We'll give everyone a free drink and biscuit."

As I'm walking across the car park a Delkim bursts into life somewhere on Willow Lake. I hurry along the muddy track. Harry and a couple of anglers from adjacent swims are standing beside Greg, a local lad who was in the year below me at school, hanging on to what is obviously a whacker. He looks nervous, glancing over his shoulder at the gathering crowd.

"Don't worry about them mate, you concentrate on getting that fish on the bank" Harry instructs, alternately supping his coffee and puffing on a large Cuban cigar. The angry fish is charging left, taking him down the margin and putting a healthy bend in the butt of his Greys Prodigy.

"I hope you've tied those bloody knots well. We don't want the bugger getting off,"

Harry says while looking round at me.

"Kes grab the net and do the honours for our guest."

"No problem."

It's not long before he has her plodding around on a short line.

"Go on lad give her the butt again!"

"Here she comes! Keep its head up! Get in there!" I shout, sweeping her up in the mesh, the first fish of the day, a beautiful pristine linear, weighing in at 35lb. Harry hands over three tenners and a fiver to the captor. Greg's grinning like a catfish now, suddenly enjoying a moment of celebrity status, and his first 30. I spread the news while gathering tea orders. By lunchtime, with two more thirties banked and several doubles from the prize fishing lake, the mood is much improved. Even the anglers on Monsters are beginning to dream again, after a couple of shows from a large mirror between the two islands.

The afternoon is quiet and wet, with anglers busy in their little green homes, drinking tea, looking, listening to the radio, and preparing for the promise of a busy night ahead.

As the light fades, we retreat from the rain on to the shop veranda where Harry is busy on the barbecue.

"Free sausage sandwiches and a bottle of beer is keeping them sweet," he says.

"Not quite the happy start were hoping for, didn't even get decent weather," Tommy says.

"We were on the telly," I say.

"True, but all they showed was that bitch swimming around my lake."

"Well, they say all publicity is good publicity," Tommy offers half-heartedly.

"Maybe, but they'll pay for ruining my day, the bastards. Hope she gets bleedin' pneumonia!"

"I wouldn't worry Harry, it'll be forgotten in a day or two. Kes is right, all it's done is given you great profile on *Look East* and *Anglia Tonight*. Imagine how much it would cost to get a two minute advert on the telly."

"I hope you're right," Harry says, a bit more cheerfully.

"Someone will get a monster in the next day or so. Marsh Lakes will be on the front of Carp-Talk all summer. You'll be booked solid," I say.

"I was surprised to see you get stuck in earlier, Kes, thought you didn't much care for Marsh Lakes," Harry says.

"Just doing my bit for the team. I love this place, the Lagoon is empty."

"That place is over-rated, all it's got is a couple of fat lumps and a handful of average back-ups. Don't know what all the fuss is about."

"I think that's a bit off the mark Harry, but if he wants to sit on the Lagoon blanking all summer, that's up to him," Tommy says.

"Can't see the appeal at all. Much rather hear those alarms going off and have a bend in my rod."

"The Lady is a national treasure Harry, a real history fish. Lots of anglers would love to catch her, including our young bivvy tramp here," Ron says.

I'm thinking *"She's worth five of the lumps in Marsh Lakes",* but not wanting to wind up Harry, keep my gob shut.

"You're living in the past Kes. Everyone can have a crack at monster fish these days. It's called progress."

"Harry has a point. How many anglers could actually fish at Redmire in its heyday, twelve? Not exactly a level playing field was it," Tommy says.

"But it had mystery and a true spirit of adventure," Ron chips in.

"I agree, and I'm not sure everyone should have the chance to catch a record fish. Shouldn't you have to earn the right?" I say.

"Bullshit. If you've got the wedge, you can have a dangle. I had you down as a socialist Kes, turns out you're Lord Snooty," Harry says.

"Money talks eh Harry?" Tommy says.

"Too right!"

"Seems to me like there's something for everyone these days. You can pick and choose your own challenge. No point getting too worked up about it, it's only fishing," Ron says.

"Blimey, that's a bit profound for you, " I say.

"Oi, watch it. Just cos I'm not gobbing off every hour of the day, like some round here, don't mean my head's empty."

"Fair point, sorry Ron," I say.

Ron's contribution to our bickering has a surprising effect. We all just sit and stare out into the darkness, listening to the rain on the shop roof, sipping beer and munching on our roasted meat. Four cave men enjoying a stone-age diet. Even Harry looks in contemplative mood.

Beeeeeeeeeeeeeeeeeeeeeeeeeeeep!

"Hey ho, this is what we've been waiting for, someone's in on Monsters," Tommy says.

We charge out into the night, shouting encouragement, carrying beers and buns. Tommy and I take the lead, jumping over puddles on the newly laid gravel path, Ron and Harry lumbering along a few yards behind. It probably takes less than a minute for us to get round the back to the Island swim, but it's clear when we arrive that all is not well. It's my new mate Steve, from the boot sale, and he's frantically wading, without waders, to his left.

"What's up son?" Harry asks

"It's got round the island. Couldn't stop it."

"I know that feeling. Is she still on?" Harry asks.

"Yeah, definitely, I can feel vibrations down the line. It's shit or bust time."

"No, hang on a minute. Don't pull for a break, just give a bit of line if you need to. I'll get the boat."

A few minutes later Harry and Steve are edging their way out to the island, under power from the electric outboard.

"Sorry chaps, Monster emergency. Fish snagged on the island," he shouts.

Lights go on and off, trees rustle, lots of shouting from Harry, and finally a call "she's free!" More fun and games, as the boat is towed to the middle of the lake.

"Can you see her?"

"I think she's under the boat in a weed bed."

"Give it some welly, she must be tiring by now."

"There she is. Blimey, it's huge!" Steve gasps.

"I've got the net"

A cry of "Oh shit" precedes an almighty splash.

"No swimming allowed Steve!" I shout.

"Shut up Kes, he's fallen in," Harry shouts.

"You do surprise me," an angler shouts from the other side of the lake.

"Can he swim?" Someone else shouts from the darkness.

In the torchlight I can see a head in the water and a hand grabbing the side of the boat. "I'm ok," Steve says.

"Have you still got the rod?" Harry asks anxiously.

"Yes, it's here," he says dragging the rod from under the water.

"Thank god for that."

Line is ripping off the spool.

"Here you take it," he says handing it up to Harry.

More banging, straining and swearing as Harry hauls him back into the boat with one hand. A few seconds break in the entertainment, and then, "it's still on," followed by cheers from the gathering crowd.

"Where is she?" Steve asks.

"Back over by the Island I think," Harry says. "Here you have this, while I get on the outboard."

"Come in number one, your time is up," I shout.

"I'd leave it Kes," Tommy whispers in my ear.

After a further five minutes or so, a head torch goes on, just out beyond where the fish was originally hooked.

"Are you winning?" Ron shouts.

"We've won!" Harry shouts back. "Looks like a real clonker, might even be the big mirror."

When they finally make it back to terra firma, poor old Steve looks a bit worse for wear. He's drenched from head to foot, his face decorated with fronds of weed. He's also shivering like a cartoon character, having been soaked to the skin for at least half an hour. On most August evenings this wouldn't have been a problem, but tonight it's more like November than holiday season. Tommy recognises the danger signs and immediately makes him strip off and get into his sleeping bag. I'm left on fish duty, holding the monster in the net while everyone dashes around trying to halt Steve's slide towards hypothermia. Ron nips off up to the shop for some dry clothes and a cup of hot sweet tea. Tommy fires up Steve's Coleman stove and shuts the bivvy door.

"I know you're pleased he's caught a Monster Tommy, but don't think he's up for a rogering right now!" I joke.

"You'll finish him off Tommy, I don't want a dead angler on my hands," Harry says.

"It's good here, more drama than an episode of Eastenders," says one of the anglers, supping his bottle of beer and obviously enjoying his first day at Marsh Lakes.

With Steve dry and sipping hot tea, we turn our attention back to the fish. I shine my head torch down into the net. Filling the entire base is a massive dark back. I lift the mesh slightly on one side, tipping the fish and revealing a glistening grey flank and a collection of scales down by the tail. I instantly know it can only be one fish, the giant mirror. We carefully put the weighsling under the net, and Ron and I place her on the mat.

"Come on Steve, get out here and have a look at this. You've got yourself the Queen of the Monsters," I say.

"Bloody hell, I've never seen anything like it. How big do you think it is?" A shaky looking Steve asks.

"Bigger than anything you ever dreamed of," I say.

"Let's just say you've smashed the British record and may even have got a new world record," Harry says proudly.

"Shit!" Steve says, which doesn't seem to quite do the moment justice, but I know what he means.

"Let's find out," Tommy says.

Minutes later Harry is firing off his camera at a new 'British record', 94lb 8oz of Hungarian common carp. Steve barely has the strength to lift it off the ground, but he looks very happy, if not a little bewildered at being the second new 'British record' holder in a week. Harry is beaming for the first time today, but later confesses to being disappointed it has gone back in weight. He was hoping it would break the 100lb barrier and set a new world record. Sadly, I have a feeling it won't be long!

Twenty-Three

Observe your enemies, for they first find out your faults.

Antisthenes, 445-365 BC

Next morning I'm woken by heavy metal rain drumming on the shop roof, mouth like a camel's arse, the pungent mix of boilies and bait dips poisoning every breath. Sleeping in the bait department wasn't such a great idea, but I drew the short straw, a night on call for any 30lb+ captures. After three hours fitful sleep am now only slightly pissed and hugely hung over. Harry, had us all up in his kitchen until the small hours celebrating the capture of the newly named 'British record', *Istvan!*

7.08 a.m. Feeling slightly better in the fresh air, curled up in my bag on the veranda, brew in hand, sunglasses on. Still raining out there in bivvy land. A hopeful grebe is hunting for its breakfast. *You're wasting your time mate, these fish are all at least 30 times bigger than you.* I sit back and run my mind over the last 24 hours. I have to admit it's been more entertaining than I imagined, TV crews, protestors swimming in the lake, and Britain's, or is that Hungary's, first 90-pounder. We seem to have skipped the first 70 and 80- pounders. We even got some dodgy video but hilarious soundtrack of the boating adventure, which I'll post up on the Marsh Lakes website and *YouTube* channel this morning. Harry was back on top form by the end of the evening, plying Steve with drinks, promising he would be a Carp-Talk cover boy next week. I'll go round and check on him in a while, he was a bit worse for wear, and had to be carried back to his bivvy at 2.30 a.m.

Ron and Tommy pull up in front of the shop while I'm still lying on the veranda.

"Morning Kes. See you're working hard. How does it feel?" Tommy asks, grinning at me through the open window of his old Astra van.

"My head? Feels pretty bad," I say.

"Not that, you beer head. I mean losing the British record after a couple of days?"

"Crikey, I hadn't even thought about it. Not proper records anyway are they."

"Listen to Mr Grumpy," Ron shouts from inside the car, "he was happy enough the other day!"

"Anyway, get off your arse, you're supposed to be patrolling the lake," Tommy says.

"I was, just finished a lap," I lie.

"Oh yeah looks like it." My dry rain jacket and trousers are draped over the chair next to me. "Funny how you managed to avoid getting a single drop of rain on those."

"Busted!"

"Again," Tommy says.

I haul myself up out of the bedchair and scramble into my Wychwood waterproofs. Looking out over the lakes I glimpse a movement over near the perimeter fence.

"I think I just saw someone taking a dump over at the back of Willow Lake," I tell Ron as he comes up the steps.

"Well go and check it out. I'll catch you up in a minute. Could be our first chance to ban someone," he says, smiling.

"Only if I actually catch them in the act, otherwise I'll have to carry it round to each swim saying, excuse me mate is this yours?"

"We'll just go round and give them all a rollocking!"

"Why don't you bring your gun with you, that will really put the wind up them!"

"Good idea!"

"Ron, I was joking. It's a fishery, not Guantanamo Bay!"

"Not when I'm on duty," Ron laughs.

Rain drops are exploding on the surface of Monsters, blurring the boundary between lake and sky. A wet suit and oxygen tank may be required to complete this round of bailiffing. Biblical flooding is looking a distinct possibility. Oh and here comes Noah in his Ark, sailing up from Earith. The water is up at least six inches on yesterday evening, and it's forecast to be heavy all day.

"Nice weather for the ducks," shouts a sheltering angler from the Shallows swim.

"Anything showing?"

"No mate, this rain has been pounding the lake all night. The fish seem to have the hump with it, like me."

"It's not too cold though, so they should have a trough sooner or later," I say encouragingly.

I see another movement out the back. "Good luck, I'll see you later."

I recognise that blue waterproof. Two figures are skulking behind the brambles between Willow and Monsters lakes. I creep up behind them.

"What the hell are you doing in here again?"

"Bloody hell Kes, you scared the life out of me," Jay says.

"Just out for a stroll on the meadows and got a bit lost, nothing wrong with that is there?" Saira replies casually, looking rather pleased with herself.

"Yeah right, didn't you cause enough grief yesterday?"

"Oh that was just the warm up act," Jay says.

"That's great news, NOT! How the hell did you get in?"

Jay grins and makes a cutting motion.

"You two really are pushing your luck. Harry will string you up if he catches you, and Ron is coming round any minute, with his shotgun!"

"Ooh I'm really scared, the postman is going to get me," Saira says.

"You're not going for a swim again are you?"

"Not today, far too cold and wet. This is just reconnaissance."

"Reconnaissance for what?"

"It's a surprise. You like surprises don't you Kes?" Saira asks.

"Not when you're involved."

"That's not very friendly."

"Since when were you interested in being friendly?"

I get the middle finger treatment, again. She really is surprisingly feral for a posh blond from Hemingford Abbots.

"You've had a good look, so you can leave now before world war three kicks off."

I point back to St, Ives, and make my *don't mess with me* face. I think it comes across more as *please leave now, you're going to get me in a whole lot of trouble*, because they both look amused and unconcerned. Ron is almost on us before they scuttle off to the fence.

"What are you up to? Ron asks. "Where's this anti-social dumper then?"

"False alarm on the turd front. Must have been someone having a slash," I say, looking over Ron's shoulder where I can see Jay and Saira waving at me as they pull back the fence wire.

"I think we can forgive the odd slash given the amount of rain coming down."

I change the subject, "thought I saw a fish in the margin."

"Fancy another foreign lump do you?"

"Nah, not really, it's not the one for me," I say glancing nervously over my shoulder, "tempting though, I'll give you that."

Jay and Saira make a run for it over the fields. Fortunately, Ron is peering into the water looking for whackers. Some security guard!

After work I take a walk into St. Ives looking for the *Heron*. I don't have to search far, it's moored on the town quay. Jay and Saira are peering at a map in the cabin with the usual suspects. Jay notices me gawping at them and comes up.

"Hi Kes, what's up, come to help us plan the next *FishAction* protest?"

"You know what's up. I want to know exactly what you have in mind."

"Saira told you earlier, it's a surprise."

"Come on, I'm worried about the Kamikaze sisterhood in there, and about you dropping me in it."

"Relax, you haven't told me anything."

"Right, you remember that when Harry comes calling, and he will."

"My lips are sealed."

"Good. Be careful, and keep that girlfriend of yours on a tight lead."

Jay is giving nothing away so I leave. Better not to be seen with them right now. I go in search of Tommy, who's tucked in his favourite corner of the Floods Tavern supping a pint of Broadside and reading Anglers Mail.

"Hello Kes, what's up, you've got a face like a wet weekend in Bognor? Here look, this'll cheer you up, you're famous!"

On the front cover is a picture of me holding the big Marsh mirror, and the headline *New Carp Record?* At least they got that right, even if it is already out of date.

"Yeah I know, I look a right dork. Has Harry seen it? He won't like the question mark," I say.

"I don't think so, he'd have been on the blower, it's just what we needed though. There's no hiding these are foreign lumps, and as you said people will be flocking to fish for them."

"Shouldn't that be shoaling to fish for them."

"Not one of your best. Come on spit it out, there's obviously something on your mind. You're not happy about this are you," he says, pointing at the picture of me on the table.

"Oh I'm not worried about that, it's quite funny really. I'm more stressed about *FishAction*."

"Relax, I've already had a word with Harry, we've upped our security status to *shoot on sight*. He's got Ron, aka the Bunnyhugger terminator, sleeping over there."

"I found them inside Marsh this morning, they're planning something else."

"Why the hell didn't you tell us?"

"Sorry Tommy, I thought I'd handle it. Don't tell Harry, he'll definitely think I'm one of them."

"And are you?"

"I can't believe you're asking me that. Of course I'm not. I just want to avoid things getting out of hand. I think Jay and Saira are out of their depth on this one. Taking on St. Ives Angling Club down the meadow is one thing, taking on Harry Plant is several leagues up."

"Ok, I won't tell Harry, but use those brains of yours, and don't try to sort out *FishAction* on your own. You look thirsty, how about a pint?"

"No Thanks. Still feeling a bit rough after last night's session, I'm off over the Lagoon to bait up and then home for an early night."

"So still on the Lady mission are you?"

"You bet."

"Good lad, I'll see you in the morning. And don't worry, it'll be fine."

I leave Tommy, pick up a St. Ives speciality, large chilli doner in nan bread, munch my way up the high street, and cross over the ring road. Normally this has a magic effect. My brain totally switches into carping mode and I'm instantly scanning for bivvies with one eye while the other monitors for signs of *Cyprinus carpio gigantica*. But the magic isn't strong tonight. The Lagoon has been spoilt by the new car park on its eastern bank, and while I can usually blank that out, tonight it just adds to my general gloomy mood. It almost feels like you're fishing in town now. Still, it's not all bad, the Lady is swimming around in front of me somewhere, and amazingly there's not another angler in sight. I sit for a while looking for signs, but the fish are keeping a low profile. A few baits fired in the channel out from the nature reserve and I'm off across the soggy fields heading for the St. Ives Boathaven and my bunk.

Twenty-Four

A fanatic is one who can't change his mind and won't change the subject.

Winston Churchill

ome at last, knackered, damp and frankly smelling a bit ripe. There's a note wedged in the door. It's from Ben the Boathaven manager saying they've loosened off the ropes, and warning me the river is expected to burst its banks by morning. Bring it on, it's one of the benefits of living on a boat, they're perfect for climate change. Not quite such good news for all the houses on the flood plain. I think about giving mum a ring to warn her, but it's 10.00 p.m., she'll be tucked up in bed by now. I can't believe it though, a flood in the middle of August. Being on the flood plain, right at the edge of what was once the great Fen, the Lagoon is one of the first lakes to suffer. Oh well, there's plenty of work to be done down at Marsh and I'm going to be doing long shifts at Tommy's in St. Ives.

A few logs in the wood burner soon warm the cabin, nothing like a night on a chair to make you appreciate your own bed. I watch the flames dance around, *must go and have a shower in a minute.* I can feel sleep coming on, mind wandering around the corners of my memory. With dad as a kid hauling from pit one at the Woolpack in Godmanchester, and then back to the present, Saira in her bikini, wow she is HOT, and very annoying. Harry is there, challenging and full of energy. Ron and Tommy too, my brothers of the angle, and always the Lady, swimming around my brain, just out of reach. *One day you'll be mine!*

Next thing I know, I'm awake and it's pitch black, no sign of the fire. *It must be late. Shit, I don't believe it, why have I woken up?* I hate waking up in the middle of the night. My mind starts racing and it takes hours to get back off to sleep. I was knackered, should have slept for England. I reach for my phone, 2.30 a.m. Outside, the sound of an engine chugging away, that must be what woke me up, the bastards. Pushing back the curtains

I can see a boat entering the lock at speed. What are they doing, the river is way too high? It's the *Heron*, Jay steering, Saira at the bow shining a torch onto the water. *Oh no, here we go! What the hell are they up to at this time?* My first reaction is to jump up and challenge them, but remembering Tommy's words, I grab the phone. *Come on mate where are you?* No answer. I leave a message, "Ron, it's Kes, get down to the back fence, I think *FishAction* are up to something." I try Tommy, no answer, and think about ringing Harry, but decide against it for now. Better find out if they're really heading for Marsh. *Of course they are, where else would they be going at this time?*

Right, I'll have to get down there. Twenty minutes later the Passat is splashing through the puddles in Marsh car park. Good, quite a few cars, plenty of back up if required. It all looks quiet, no lights on, but better have a look round before waking Harry and Ron. I already know where they'll come in, so make my way down between Monsters and Willow lakes, heading for the fence behind the Islands swim. If they're coming they picked a bloody awful night for it, the rain is hacking down the Ouse valley bringing half the Atlantic ocean with it. Through the darkness I can just see some movement, and then as I get closer, hear voices whispering. It's them alright! Just inside the fence someone is blowing up a dinghy, Saira's mate Danny I think. Three others figures are huddled round, hoods up heads down, one tall, two smaller with rucksacks on their backs.

"Someone's coming!" A flashlight hits my face, dazzling me.

"It's alright, it's only Kes again. Don't they ever let you go home?" Jay asks, sounding surprisingly relaxed.

"You better clear off NOW!"

"Too late for that, we're moving in," Saira says.

"What, you're joking. I don't believe it, you've gone way too far this time!"

"We've only just begun."

"Carpenters 1970," I blurt out. My brain is hard wired for pop trivia even at the least appropriate moments.

"You really are the village idiot aren't you," Saira sneers.

I try to explain, but understandably they seem to be in quite a hurry, and I really ought to be raising the alarm.

"OK, we're set," Danny says, "let's go!"

They pick up the boat, and I put myself between them and the lake.

"What are you going to do?" I ask.

"Isn't it obvious, we're setting up a protest camp on the island!" Jay says.

Of course, it's Jane's speciality, living up trees for weeks on end.

"Out of the way Kes, you can't stop us," Saira says aggressively.

"We'll see about that!"

Time to call in the troops. I start shouting trying to wake up all the anglers on site, and see a few lights coming on as I race back round to the shop.

"Wake up Ron, we've got trouble!" I shout, banging on the door. A sleepy face appears.

"Sorry, I was away with the fairies. What are you doing here? Has someone caught a whacker?" Ron asks, looking confused.

"No mate, *FishAction* are here!"

"Yeah good one, in the middle of the night, you're joking right?"

"Do I sound like I'm joking?"

"Shit, you go and get Harry, while I get the gun."

Harry appears at his front door, wearing a grim face and blue and white striped pyjamas. I quickly explain the situation, provoking an explosion of expletives and flurry of activity in the hall of the mock mansion. He grabs a Barbour, stamps his feet into Hunter wellies, then selects a twelve bore and box of cartridges from the back of the cloakroom. Loading up the gun, he steps out onto the porch beside me, and without warning gives it both barrels into the night sky! He then charges off down the lawn, shouting "you bastards are trespassing and I'm going to shoot the lot of you."

"Ron, we're being invaded," Harry shouts, as he gallops past the shop, "bring your gun!"

"I've got it. We'll scare the living daylights out of them!"

"I'll do more than that!" He says, rushing ahead. "If they think they can squat here they've got another thing coming."

Out in the lake a light is shining on the island, but someone is still in the Island swim. Harry gets there first.

"What the hell are you doing on my land?" He says, and smashes the stock of his gun into their face. They fall down onto their knees and he puts a size ten into their guts.

"Harry, stop!" A low groan comes from the slumped figure. I shine my head torch at them. It's Jay, blood splattered across his face.

"He's busted my nose," Jay groans.

"Just stay down or he'll give you another kicking," I whisper.

But Harry is off, racing round the lake to where his boat is moored. The land battle is over, but the battle for Monsters island is about to begin.

"Tell them to quit Jay, the girls are going to get hurt."

"What Saira, Jane and Danny, no chance. This was their idea, they've been planning it for weeks."

Ron arrives. "I've called the police."

"Good idea. Look at the state of Jay!" I say.

"Tough. He had it coming."

"It's out of order."

"I know, but they should have thought about that before they broke in."

Another blast of the shotgun pierces through the stormy night sky.

"He'll bloody kill someone in a minute," Jay says.

"I did warn you. Get out while you've got the chance," I say.

"No way, I'm waiting for the police."

Ron shines his flashlight across the water. In the beam we can see Saira and Jane climbing up the big willow. Harry is just approaching the island, and as he cruises into shore he bellows, "come down now you little shits, or you'll get an arse full of lead shot!"

"Sod off, we're staying here until they close you down for smuggling and torturing fish."

" I think you'll find you're the ones breaking the law, you hippy bitch."

Harry jumps out of the boat and charges into the undergrowth towards the willow where Saira and Jane are perched, and that Danny is frantically climbing. The gun goes off again.

"Aaaarrggghhh, he's shot me," Danny yells.

"Harry, what the hell are you doing? That's enough, the police are coming," Ron shouts from the Islands Swim.

"Get down now, or you'll get some more of the same," Harry says.

"That's attempted murder, you'll get locked up for that," Saira shrieks.

"Jay, call an ambulance for Danny," Jane shouts across the lake.

"Jay can't do anything right now. I'll do it," I call out.

Danny is lying at the base of the tree beside Harry, who is ignoring his cries, and concentrating on trading insults and threats with Saira and Jane. There are lights shining onto the island from every angle as the anglers try to get a view of the drama raging before their bleary and startled eyes. Harry emerges from the trees and gets back in the boat. I feel relieved, maybe he's finally seen sense and is coming back for medical supplies, for help to get Danny off the island.

"Harry calm down, it's getting way out of hand," Ron says.

"They started it, and I'll teach them they can't mess with me."

"What are you doing?" I ask.

"I'm going to get my chainsaw, they're coming down one way or another."

Harry has totally lost the plot, and he's bringing in new weaponry to end the battle. Danny is lucky to be alive and now Saira and Jane are in his firing line.

"Harry, the police are on their way," I say.

"Who bleedin' well called them, we can deal with this ourselves."

"Harry, how badly hurt is Danny?" I ask.

"Oh it's Danny is it? Bit familiar with this lot aren't you?" He says, eyes staring wildly into mine, spittle in each corner of his mouth, hot breath on my wet face. "He'll live, but won't be sitting down for a while," a hint of a smile in his eyes amongst the red mist.

"They're kids Harry, filling them full of lead isn't going to help," I plead.

"I don't need a lecture from you, they've pushed me too far."

Harry arrives back with the chain saw, and despite both of us urging him not to, he jumps in the boat. There's a pause in the action. I catch a few glimpses in the moving torch light of Danny lying holding his leg, and Saira hanging out of the tree talking to him. Then the chain saw bursts into life, and we hear the girls screaming as steel bites into wood. Fortunately Harry is not much of a lumberjack and the saw quickly jams in the trunk and stalls. Blue flashing lights appear at the gate, the police are here. I run up to let them in.

"Alright son, what's going on?"

"Animal rights protestors. It's all kicking off down there. The owner, Harry, is out on the Island trying to get them out of a tree."

"And who are you?"

"Kes Waterman, I work here."

The sound of Harry's shotgun rattles round the fishery again.

"Bloody hell, who was that? Jim, call for armed back up."

"It's Harry. He's lost it!"

"Have the protestors got weapons?"

"I don't think so."

He grabs a megaphone from the back seat, and we leg it down to the lake, splashing through puddles and mud. Ron and a few of the anglers have moved round to the point swim for a better view of the drama unfolding.

"Only the second night open, and you've had two protests, a record carp, a shooting and a broken nose. Never knew fishing here would be so much fun," says one of the anglers.

"Mr Plant, this is the police. Please come over, so we can discuss the situation."

"I'm not leaving until I've got them down and off my land," Harry shouts back.

"Is there another boat?" asks the officer, "looks like it could be a long shift!"

Ron and I get the rowing boat from Willow Lake, bale it out, and launch it into Monsters. The two officers set off into the night armed with a pair of oars and two truncheons. Jay is suffering, his nose is a mess, the shock and pain has made him puke. For the second night running Ron goes on a medical mission for hot drinks and warm clothing.

Eventually the police convince Harry to leave the island peacefully if not willingly, minus his shotgun, and chainsaw still wedged in the trunk of the willow. As they lead him away to cool down in a patrol car, he hisses at Ron "Get Tommy out here, I want those slags out of that tree tonight, and I don't care how you do it."

"No one's going onto that island without my permission," the officer says.

"Ruddy marvellous, can't even deal with trespassers on your own land these days."

"You can't go round shooting people Mr Plant."

"It was self-defence."

"We'll let the judge decide about that."

And off he goes, trudging through the mud, angry and unrepentant, in his soggy blue and white striped pyjamas.

Half an hour later Ron and I are struggling with the paramedics to get a pale, bloody and semi-conscious Danny into the slippery boat and off the island. He leaves Marsh Lakes face down in the ambulance clutching a big red patch on the back of his thigh. Jays goes with him nursing a swollen, crooked nose and a nasty gash on his forehead.

"Two down, two still standing," I whisper to Ron as we watch the ambulance speed off up the lane. We shut the gate and head back down to the lake, the rain hissing and steaming in the shop floodlights.

"You've got to hand it to them. They've got balls this lot!"

"Yes, but the Kamikaze squad up our tree are ball free. It's war Ron, but not as we know it!"

"Very good, very good, it's the way you tell 'em! But what happens now?"

"I suppose we wait. The siege of Marsh Lakes is underway," I say.

Ron and I are left standing with a bunch of bemused, bedraggled anglers, and a couple of women sitting up a tree. Tommy has missed the whole thing, no doubt tucked up in a warm bed, mobile off, pushing out the zzzs, dreaming of monster carp.

"Blimey, that's come up fast," Ron says, pointing eastwards, out across the meadows.

A grey light spreading across the big fen sky reveals a new day and a new look to the Ouse Valley, the river doing its best impression of the North Sea. There's water everywhere stretching off into the distance. It's bizarre, we often see this in the winter, but I've never seen it like this in the middle of summer.

"Lucky we got that bund in when we did," I say.

"If we get much more of this wet stuff, we'll need more than a bund, we'll need a sea wall. It'll be flooded all the way out to Kings Lynn."

"I'd better get back to the Boathaven and check the *Kingfisher*. What should we do about Saira and Jane?"

"Oh leave 'em there for now, they ain't going anywhere, and I can't see what harm they'll do. Well it's 5 o'clock lads, breakfast time. Anyone fancy a tea and a bacon sarnie, on the house?"

Back at the Boathaven, the riverside moorings are underwater. I borrow a tender and row my way out to the *Kingfisher*, which is leaning over at an alarming angle. Out in the main current, the water looks like boiling chocolate, swirling and surging over the top of the sluice gates and straight through the open lock. I can see the west corner of the Lagoon is flooded as usual. It's the worst time of year for it to happen, when the fish are so active. They'll be in that corner nosing around. Her ladyship has already had one spell in the river, and if the water goes over the low fence, we could be in trouble, but nothing I can do it about it now. One last check of the ropes and I slip down into the cabin. *Now where was I before I was rudely woken?*

Twenty-Five

If you're going through hell, keep going.

Winston Churchill

unchtime, in the cabin listening to the radio, half-heartedly tying up a few rigs and mulling over the events of last night. Harry was well out of order, and Saira and Jane are like a couple of Lara Crofts. Can't believe people are getting shot over fishing. What's going on, nothing's really happened round here my whole life, and now it's gone crazy. Through the window it looks like a scene from *Waterworld*. I'm hoping the Lagoon will still be fishable this week. Sodding typical, just when I had started to get things going down there, spots primed, ready for harvesting. I'm torn, should I fish and risk getting flooded out, or sit here waiting and brooding. To be honest, I don't really feel like fishing right now, time for another brew. I feel safe and secure in *Kingfisher*, but outside the world looks wet and scary.

What if *FishAction* actually pull it off, manage to convince people about a ban? They did it with fox hunting. We'd all look pretty pathetic if we just sat in our bivvies ignoring the threat. The British love animals, particularly if they've got big eyes, fur or feathers. I can't see them getting worked up about maggots and fish though. Maybe you need legs to win public sympathy, no that can't be right, they'll surely never ban cruelty to ants. Everyone has a right to stop those little buggers invading your kitchen. What if it becomes illegal to eat meat? Compulsory vegetarianism, blimey Morrissey would be well chuffed. Nah, we'll always be allowed to angle for fish we're going to eat, all you game and sea anglers can relax. Not so sure about coarse fishing though, or am I going soft?

My mind wanders. It's the 21st Century and *The times they are a changin*! We'll live to 150, be wired up to our computers, have designer babies and god knows what else. People have lost contact with nature. Putting food on the table means nipping down the supermarket. What do you mean sausages are minced up pig? Disgusting. Chips are made from potatoes, which grow in the ground? You're having a laugh. Not us though, carp fishing strips off the thin veneer of modern life. Using ancient skills and instinct, we employ the latest technology to hunt down, trap and subdue the mighty *Cyrpinus Carpio*. We're in tune with nature, part of the landscape. I reckon we need to encourage fishing, not ban it, get all those urban dwellers outside, away from their TVs and computer screens. The real greenies wear camo and live in bivvies. Well it would be nice to think so, but the reality is some way short. It dawns on me that too many anglers don't appreciate or value the wildlife around them! I'm afraid though, when it comes to tufties, cormorants, otters and other annoying aquatic critters we'll always struggle to appreciate them the way others do.

My mobile rings. "Kes, it's Jay."

"Hello Jay, I was just thinking about you lot. How's the nose?"

"Bloody sore, and I've got concussion. They want to keep me in for observation. I know this is a cheek, but Saira called and said the *Heron* is leaning over, could you sort it out for me?"

"You've got more front than Blackpool, after the grief you caused last night."

"I know, I wouldn't ask, but you know what you're doing and I can't think of anyone else who could get to her."

"Well Low Road is totally flooded, it's pretty much all river round here today."

"Shit, I'm already regretting last night, I don't want to lose the *Heron* too."

"*Kingfisher* was leaning right over when I got back this morning."

"That's comforting."

"Look I'll see what I can do, and give you a buzz later."

"Thanks Kes!"

"You owe me big time for this!"

I take my tender up to the marina shop, and just keep going straight into the car park. The prop starts to grind on the gravel as I attempt a turn into Low Road. No, can't just boat my way along the road to Fenstanton. Opposite, the VW garage has Ouse water lapping at the doors of its shiny new models. Climate change 1 Vorpsrung durch technik 0. The old Passat is looking a bit vulnerable, better move it. I tie the tender to the tow bar, and try turning her over, Bingo. Ben has his lads stacking sand bags in front of the shop doors. I park up on the grass slope.

"Hi Ben, global warming eh, don't you love it?"

"Nightmare mate. Should be our busiest month of the year and it feels like the middle of winter."

"Hope it doesn't come up that far," I say pointing at the sand bags.

"Just a precaution, but we have been flooded out before. What are you up to?"

"Oh we had a bit of excitement down at the new lakes last night," I say and explain the full drama that unfolded while everyone else was sleeping. "And now I need to get back down there."

"Bit tricky mate, we're cut off at the moment," Ben says.

"I don't really fancy heading out into the main current with this small electric outboard. I need something with a bit more poke."

"I've got an outboard you can use in the workshop."

A few minutes later I'm rigged up with an old 40hp Johnson outboard that Ben says will probably get me airborne if I open her up.

A few warm up laps round the marina, and yes, I am definitely over-gunned, but it has plenty of poke for the dealing with the raging river. My courage evaporates at the Boathaven entrance, and I nervously coax her out into the main current. *Mistake, should have hit it at speed!* Swept rapidly down towards the lock, crashing into the brick walls, bumping and grinding my way through, boat spat out into the swirling torrent of the weir pool. *Shite, that was well hairy! Time to test this baby out!* Half throttle, and I'm holding my position, facing back up stream, and then throwing the engine round, speeding down towards Holywell, *king of the river!* The rain has stopped and there's a strange yellow sphere in the bright blue sky. Five disappointingly uneventful minutes later and I'm lurking in the lee of a big alder opposite the Marsh Lakes perimeter fence. A few yards upstream, the *Heron* is swaying about in the current, looking decidedly precarious. I move out into the current and approach her from downstream, using her bulk to provide some shelter. The mooring ropes are tied to stakes well below the surface and out of reach. I'll have to get some more rope, tie her to the fence and then cut the original rope. The look on Ron and Tommy's faces is priceless as I motor round the perimeter fence, waving at them. The water is up at the top of the bund, a few more inches and it will start pouring into Marsh Lakes.

"Traded the Passat for a more suitable model, cars are so 20th century!" I shout.

"You nut job," Ron shouts back.

I tie the boat up to the outside of the fence, run up the slope and round to the main gate. There are a few journalists hovering around, but I show my pass to the two coppers on guard and enter without a word.

"See we've got company."

"Yeah, the press are pissed off because Tommy won't let them in and we won't tell them anything," Ron says.

"No one's coming on site until I hear from Harry," Tommy says.

"You missed an action packed night." I say.

"Your school mates are total nutters aren't they?"

"Harry did a good impression of Jack Nicholson in The Shining while we're talking of nutters. And they're not my mates. Danny and Saira always were a nightmare, campaigning about this and that. I can't quite believe Jay is mixed up in it though. He was Mr nice guy at school, reading books and writing poetry."

"He'll have something to write about now. Trouble is, it will go in the newspaper," Ron says.

"Where are all the anglers?" I ask.

"I've shut the lakes. Can't have people trying to fish while the sisters of mercy are out there," Tommy says.

"Can't believe how much the water has come up since this morning."

"Yeah I know, it's got to be about three feet," Ron says.

"We're sitting here keeping an eye on it."

"It's certainly a bit dangerous out there, the current is really strong right up to the fence."

"I know, hope they did a good job tying in that bund or the whole lot could get washed away."

"The forecast is for more rain tonight."

"I heard on the radio, it could be worse than the flood of 1947!"

"Now you're here Kes, can you give me a hand repairing the fence?" Ron says.

"No worries, and Jay rang, asked me to sort out the *Heron*. I need some ropes. Have we got any?"

"What and you said yes?"

"Well, I don't like the thought of the *Heron* sinking," I say.

"No more than they deserve," Tommy says.

"Probably not, but all the same."

"We've got loads of rope in the workshop.".

"Right lads I'm off up to the St. Ives shop, sort a few things out and put a notice on the door. I don't think we'll open for a couple of days," Tommy says.

With Tommy gone we kick back, time for a quick brew to go with the regulation afternoon Eccles cakes, chew over the battle for Marsh Lakes, and what we should do with our uninvited guests. Ron reckons they'll be off within 24 hours, but I'm not so sure. Jane lasted weeks on the meadow. Ron tells me Georgia has gone to her mothers, she's so upset and annoyed with Harry. An hour later and suitably fortified I go off in search of rope while Ron gathers a selection of tools and some fencing material. I then head back round to the tender and fire up the outboard. Ron puts on his waders and wanders down to the fence at the back of Monsters. I can hear him exchanging a few words with the girls.

"You should bloody see yourselves ladies. Sitting up that tree in the middle of a flood."

"Take a look in the papers tomorrow, and you'll see who's winning hearts and minds," Saira shouts.

"Yeah whatever darlin', remember we've got the law on our side," Ron replies.

"Tell that to your boss, when he's banged up for shooting Danny," Jane says.

"And by the way we're going to sort out the *Heron* for you," I say, from the other side of the fence.

"Not that you deserve it," Ron adds.

"Thanks," Saira says.

"Sorry didn't hear that, can you say it a bit louder," I say.

"Up yours!"

"She's all charm this one isn't she," Ron says, shaking his head.

Ron squeezes through the gap in the fence, and carefully steps down off the bund to just above the waist of his waders. The water is flowing quite swiftly even though we're 20m from the actual river channel. He ties one rope to the bow of the *Heron* and attaches it to the nearest of the Marsh fence posts, and then does the same on the stern. I'm sitting in the tender hanging on to the original stern rope, which is taut as a bowstring, waiting for the instruction to cut it. When I do the *Heron* lurches around dangerously in the strong current.

"Right, now do the front one, but watch out it could whack into you," Ron says, moving back holding onto the fence by the boat's stern.

I hack into the rope with my fishing knife, and suddenly it gives. The *Heron* lurches upright and sweeps round, trapping me between it and the fence. There is a nasty crunch as I'm squashed against the wire, but on the rebound I manage to blast my way out into the main current.

"That was bloody dangerous," I shout out to Ron, holding my position mid-river.

"You all right?"

"Yeah I'm fine. Do you think it's safe now?"

"Yeah should be, but I'll go down and just shorten those ropes a bit. Can you nip back to the workshop, I've left the fence ties on the bench."

"Alright, won't take long." I open up the throttle. "Watch this beauty take off."

I'm only in the workshop for a couple of minutes but as I come back out I hear shouting. It's Saira and Jane up in the trees. *What the hell are they on about now?* There is urgency in their voices, but I can't make out what they're saying. Running, then sprinting round to the boat, clambering in, a wave of panic. Something's happened. Looking for anything obvious, nothing, all seems calm.

"Hurry up Kes," Jane shouts.

"What's happened?" I shout.

"Over there, quick," she says, pointing.

Saira is already out of the tree and swimming across Monsters. Hang on, where's Ron. I shout his name, scanning the river, looking up the fence line. Saira pushes through the fence and grabs hold of the tender.

"He was just sorting out the ropes on the *Heron* for you."

"I know, I saw him go Kes."

"GO, go where?"

"IN, he fell in!"

"Where is he? I can't see him. Quick get in the boat."

"He was wearing waders wasn't he? Saira asks.

"Yes."

"We haven't got long. He's in trouble Kes."

I know it, but can't speak.

Saira and I scan the river, peering into the muddy water, motoring down stream, looking for any sign of Ron's massive frame. *This can't be happening, I mean it doesn't happen, not here.*

"Kes, look, up there, I think I can see something."

Wedged against a bush, face down, arms outstretched. Shouting now, dragging, heaving, too heavy. Lifting his head, unconscious, eyes closed. Holding him to the side of the boat, while Saira takes us back upstream towards the nearest land. "Careful, not too fast," I say.

Sloshing through the water, both of us hauling Ron onto the muddy bank.

"Call for an ambulance Kes."

Saira takes control, tilting his head back, checking for breath, mouth to mouth, no pulse. Pressing down on his chest repeatedly, then mouth to mouth again. Nothing. Again and again Saira pumps on his chest and breathes for Ron.

"Wake up Ron!" I shout, holding his wet, limp hand. Saira is exhausted, face red and sweaty, cheeks and hands smeared with mud. "Keep going Saira, please keep going."

"Watch me, you have to take over"

"I don't think I can."

"Of course you bleeding can, watch what I'm doing."

"Where the hell is the ambulance?"

Saira moves out of the way, I kneel by Ron's head feeling sick, unsure of what to do. Saira talks me through it, pressing down on his chest, desperately trying to get his circulation going. My mouth against his, breathing for him, his chest rising and falling. Checking for breath, nothing. We keep going, swapping every five minutes, not talking, occasionally stealing anxious glances at each other, both knowing it is futile, but neither willing to accept Ron's fate. My attempts become more and more frantic, and Saira keeps telling me to keep a steady rhythm. A siren in the distance, getting louder, at last, someone else to take over, to tell us it's ok to stop. When they finally make it to us, we both sit back on our knees, staring at Ron's lifeless body lying in the mud. His once powerful frame drained of all its energy, his red and lively face, now pale and expressionless. Saira takes my hand in hers, my head bowed, eyes closed, holding back the tears. "I'm so sorry Kes!"

It's not long before the journalists arrive, having followed the ambulance, barging around trying to get shots and footage, the paramedics shouting at them to back off. Saira agrees to be interviewed by BBC Look East, while I hang back trying not to draw attention but listening to what she is saying. She makes a few comments on the protest, but mostly talks about how Ron had been trying to save the *Heron*, how it happened, that he fell over and was swept away by the strong current. After the interview she comes over to me. "Come on Kes let's get out of here."

There's no one around when we get back to the shop. Well there wouldn't be. Harry's in the police cells, Georgia's away, Tommy's at the shop in St. Ives and Ron's dead. It feels awful even thinking it, like it's something I dreamt, or an alternative reality I created in some horrendous mental ramble. Jane has left the tree and joined us on the veranda. Saira is kitted out in various branded carp clothes from the shop, which is way too weird! And here we are, sitting around drinking tea at Marsh Lakes, two Bunnyhuggers and a headbanging bivvy tramp! No one says anything. What can you say? Suddenly we can hear gushing water, like someone turned on a huge tap.

"Oh my god, look at that," Jane says, pointing towards the fence.

Water is pouring through the bund, and as we stare more and more of it crumbles away, the brown muddy river surging in staining the clear lake water.

"Bloody Hell" is all I can manage.

We sit there for the best part of an hour watching as slowly the individual lakes disappear, swallowed up by the river. The fence is left hanging, a huge gap where the bund has been eroded away.

"So much for Marsh Lakes. They're gone now," I say.

"Will the fish escape?" Jane asks.

"I reckon."

Eventually, Saira announces that she's going, Jane agrees. The protest is over!

Tommy is locking up the shop on the High Street when I get there. I try to get it out, but no words come. Tommy stares. Last time it was dad and now it's Ron.

"Kes, what's wrong?"

"It's Ron. He fell in the river."

"The silly bugger."

"He's drowned!"

"Kes, you shouldn't joke about things like that."

I just stand there, tears welling up. Tommy can see this is no wind up.

"What... how?"

"We were trying to save the *Heron* and fix the fence. I went back for a few more bits. He must have tripped or slipped."

"But Ron's a good swimmer."

"I know but he was wearing his waders, and I think once the water filled them the current just swept him down and away. He didn't stand a chance."

Tommy sinks down onto the step of the shop and puts his head in his hands. We go over the road into the Royal Oak. Tommy has a brandy, but I can't stomach anything. I just keep seeing Ron's face wet, muddy and lifeless. I tell him about the way Saira tried to save him. Tommy points out that if it wasn't for *FishAction* there wouldn't have been a boat to save or a hole in the fence to mend, and none of this would have happened.

"I wish Harry had never come in the shop. I wish he never bloody dug Marsh Lakes. It's caused nothing but grief."

"You can't blame Harry."

"It's not just Harry, it's everything, Ron, dad, *FishAction*. It's a bloody mess and I'm sick of it. I just want it to be how it was before."

"You've had a rough year."

"Even the Lagoon is wrecked, with that new car park."

Tommy changes the conversation to Saira and Jane. I tell him they've abandoned their protest. Then we see it on the pub television. It feels unreal, like someone else, not us, not our lives, not our Ron, pictures of him being taken away by the paramedics, an interview with Saira, me in the background.

"Look at the state of Marsh," Tommy says, "all that work we put in getting it ready, and look at it now. You can't even see where one lake ends and the next begins."

"The monsters, 30s, and pasty commons, will all be mixed up now," I say.

"I wonder how many have escaped through that hole in the fence?"

"All of them I hope!"

It's dark when we emerge from the pub. Tommy gives me a hug and then trudges off up the High Street. I head back along the quay and lean on the railings. Gazing down into the swirling water as it surges through the sandstone arches, wisps of steam rising up off the floodlights. The bridge at St. Ives is a magical place you can feel the power of 600 years of river life, all those people who have looked out on St. Ives from here, lived their fenland lives. I find it very comforting. It feels like home, it is home. I was in this exact spot, the night I got the news about Dad being killed in Afghanistan. He was always talking about life and death. I suppose it was his way of preparing me. *Shit happens, get over it!* And *live each day as if it were your last!* He was right you have to keep on living, even if you don't think you can at the time. I loved our chats, while we were fishing. Angling and philosophy were made for each other. Ron didn't agree, my psycho-babble drove him mad, and the more he bit, the more I'd do it. We all enjoyed our top fives though, and even though I was always taking the piss, he taught me a lot about carp fishing. I can't believe he's gone!

Part Three

This royal throne of kings, this scepter'd isle,

This earth of majesty, this seat of Mars,

This other Eden, demi-paradise,

This fortress built by Nature for herself

Against infection and the hand of war,

This happy breed of men, this little world,

This precious stone set in the silver sea,

Which serves it in the office of a wall,

Or as a moat defensive to a house,

Against the envy of less happier lands,

This blessed plot, this earth, this realm, this England...

William Shakespeare, Richard ll, 1595

Twenty-Six

So if I were to give one piece of advice it would be simply this. Always keep an open mind and be willing to learn. But above all enjoy yourself, and as the man once said, "Don't forget to smell the flowers along the way."

Rod Hutchinson

I've been away for a few weeks, out of circulation. After Ron's funeral, I just went back to Kingfisher, untied and set off down river in the flood, eventually ending up beyond Ely, right in the heart of the fens. It's totally awesome, if you like big skies and a flat watery landscape. On the other hand if you want lonely and depressing you can find that too. When the skies are grey and it's blowing a hoolie from the north, it's bleak, and perfect. The weird thing about being on the river in the fens is it's higher than the surrounding land. There are huge banks obscuring your view of the countryside, and every now and then you get a glimpse of the endless dark fields stretching off to the horizon 20ft below you. It's topsy-turvy land, no hills and the rivers higher than the fields!

It took a couple of weeks before I went near my tackle. Spent ages just lying in bed, and found a day goes pretty quickly in the company of an iPod, TV and laptop. My PB was three days, just getting up to go to the loo, and make tea and toast. When I eventually surfaced I rang mum, who sounded worried. She must have spoken to Tommy, because he came up and found me the day after. I could tell by the look on his face that he was worried too. He asked if I thought I was depressed, and suggested a trip to the doctor. I laughed a lot, which got him even more twitchy. I'm not depressed. Anyone would feel a bit gloomy if their mate drowned and they found them face down in the river, if their dad got killed in some crazy war on the other side of the world, and a bunch of people from your school were trying to ban the thing you most love doing. It's normal to feel shit when shit happens. Inside I knew I was alright, it just didn't look like it to the rest of the world. My hair was getting matted and greasy, I hadn't shaved for two weeks, and frankly I was starting to smell a bit.

So, yes, mildly depressed maybe, but nothing to worry about. In fact, quite a good sign. In touch with my feelings, and thinking, always thinking. Lots of questions. What's right, what's wrong? What's cool, what's not? What's good, bad, right and wrong? It can wear you out. It's very confusing. It's hard being a thinker and some days I wish I wasn't, that I could just turn my mind off. I envy people who can sit by their rods and think about nothing, enjoy being there and soak up the day second by second. I seem to be wired a bit differently, permanently switched on, or asleep. For the last couple of weeks, in between the thinking, I've been awake but in sleep mode, consciously trying to reboot, defragment my hard disk, checking for system errors.

It's so easy spending your time doing nothing, I'm amazed more people don't do it. You just slow down and fill the day with things everyone else tries to do as quickly as possible, getting up, having breakfast, doing the shopping, that kind of thing. I got into a routine of waking up around 11.00 a.m., making a brew, listening to music, and then trudging down to the local shop in Stretham for a few bits and bobs. The village pub was quiet, so I got into sitting in there, nursing a pint and reading one of the boot-haul carp magazines until about two. The locals propping up the bar were mildly suspicious of the newly arrived long-haired, camo wearing delinquent, but after a shower, shampoo, shave, and a week of good behaviour I was labelled harmless and accepted. After my pint I'd walk back along the river to the mooring, drink more tea and watch DVDs on my laptop. That was pretty much a whole day filled up. And I realised, to my surprise, I was quite happy on my own, a natural hermit!

Anyway, last week, walking back from the pub on a lovely autumn afternoon, I stopped by a couple of willows about a quarter of a mile from the *Kingfisher*. One of them had fallen over at some point, and created a very carpy-looking snag in an otherwise straight, barren stretch. I was sure if there were any carp around they would pitch up here at some point. With that in mind I started buying a few cans of Jolly Green Giant, and sprinkling the golden grains under the overhanging branch. At first it was just skimmers and a few tench polishing off my offerings, but this afternoon everything changed. As I approached the tree, there was a big swirl. I waited for the pesky coot to bob back up again, but nothing emerged. For the first time in weeks I could feel the carp fever kicking in. Creeping along the branch, I peered down into the water. Even before dropping my Polaroids down over my eyes, it was obvious the two dark shapes below me were not *tincas*, these were big *Cypries*. I estimated one to be around the 20lb mark, pretty average stamp for the Ouse, a very lean long river common. The other fish was quite different, much deeper and broader, a slate grey, sparsely scaled mirror of around 35lb. Possibly a recent flood escapee, but a proper lump all the same.

I ran, or maybe even skipped like a girl, back to the *Kingfisher*, and began throwing gear out onto the bank. Instant cure, the fires burning again! I was going fishing, and it felt good! The next 15 minutes were a complete frenzy of activity. I was totally in the in the zone, adrenalin surging through my body again. Hands shaking, tying an eight-inch Combi-link rig with a size 10 Korda Wide Gape, attaching a couple of niblets of plastic corn to the Hair. Rod, net, mat, weighsling, rucksack, check, everything present and correct, all systems go. *Houston we are ready for lift off!* Quick march, back up the bank to the willows, and then a moment of maturity, before creeping into position, I remembered to check the line, hook and all my knots. My fishing head was back on!

I waited and watched, looking for an opportunity to drop the rig into position. The fish were active, doing circuits of their snaggy home, in other words catchable. I was determined not to blow this chance, and sat tucked in against the horizontal trunk, its branches trailing in the water to my right. To the left the second willow created a shaded canopy, but it was clear water. Sunlight was streaking in through the yellowing leaves, just enough to make out a sandy area where I had been dropping in my carp snacks. A handful of niblets were carefully lobbed onto the dinner plate. The common drifted in from the left and hovered above the baited area. It went round again, but this time swam straight down, hoovering its way through afternoon tea. The mirror was a bit more cautious, hanging back. I decided I really wanted the big girl. It was another 15 minutes before she eventually got her head down too. Bingo! During this time a plan developed. I would drop in the rig when they were safely out of the way, and then creep along to the left. This would give me a bit more leverage to get the hooked fish moving away from certain disaster if, or rather when, it bolted under the trunk and into the sunken branches. It would be shit or bust tactics, but confidence was high in the GR500 22lb braid, perfect string for the job.

Just after the mirror left the spot, the rig and more freebies were lowered. A careful shuffle left, line sunk, clutch tight, rod between my legs, hand on knee poised for action, trap set. Now it was a 50/50 chance, mirror or common. Or nothing, or tench, or bream, but that would be this morning's Kes, the new Kes, this afternoon's Kes was 100% sure it was going to be one of the carp. *A monster chance!* What a treat, unknown carp, no other angler in sight. It felt great, the fish were perfect, they kept coming round, I could see them clearly, every little movement of their fins. They were relaxed, moving confidently, excited by the little golden grains. And then it did happen, both down on the spot together. My eyes darting between the fish and the braid dangling from tip eye. For a few seconds, nothing, *come on surely you can see it, right there in front of you.* A little movement, the merest flick where the braid entered the river, then everything tight, the rod tip moving, my hand grabbing the reel, a big boil in the water, the rod wrenched round to its test curve, me hanging on, the fish accelerating with warp power. *Oh boy, I've missed this, big time!* I was laughing, pure excitement and shock at connecting with this wild creature lurking in a fenland wonderland.

The beast tried to rip my arm off, but I gave her the full treatment and feeling the unforgiving power of my Gardner string, my JRC steel and Greys Carbon, it hesitated and went for plan B, out into open water, and certain defeat in Man versus Fish contest. Everything was sweet, I'm the river snag king. She veered left, powering downstream, but I was in control, giving and taking line at will. I coaxed her back towards the willow and she came up gulping at the surface, over the net cord, beaten. I fell onto my knees staring down at the magnificent hard-fighting Cambridgeshire common carp in the margins, "*just what the doctor ordered*!" I didn't take her out of the water, but held her, just gently feeling her scales, talking to her. Finally she'd had enough, and bolted strongly, straight down into the snag. I sent Tommy a text, *coming back to town in a couple of days, see you then. The bitch is back! Elton John. Kes XX*

Twenty-Seven

*I'd fished an incredible amount of time, gone though heartaches, lost fish,
and jealousy... Now for this brief moment I had Bazil. I just held her in the
water and felt her gill covers going in and out against my hand.*

Rob Maylin, *Bazil's Bush*, 1993

8.00 a.m., a knock on the window, "Oi Oi is anything alive in there?"

It's the unmistakable vibrations of Tommy Tindall, renowned fenland tackle shop proprietor and carp hauler extraordinaire. I poke my head out on a bright but chilly morning at St. Ives Quay.

"Morning Tommy, fancy a brew?"

Tommy looks a bit hesitant, last time he saw the *Kingfisher* galley it was clearly a major health hazard inhabited by Stig of the Dump.

"It's alright, I've had a good clean up, the cups are clean, the milk's fresh."

"Blimey that's a relief. Like the new hair cut."

"Oh yeah, the squaddie look, not very heavy metal, but a lot easier for a bivvy tramp to manage."

"And you don't smell!"

I jump forward and shove my arm pit in Tommy's face. "What, are you the shower police? You fascist!" I shout, laughing.

Tommy gets me in a headlock. "It's good to see you've got your bounce back Tigger, now say sorry."

"Ok sorry!" I shout as Tommy squeezes my neck.

"So, when did the bounce return?"

"It took a while. Sort of needed to let everything swill around in my brain for a few weeks. Finding some clonking big carp to fish for out there helped a lot."

"Yeah that sounded pretty special. Did you get that big mirror?"

"Sure did."

"How big?"

"Don't know, I've given up the numbers thing."

"Bullshit!"

"Seriously, I didn't weigh it."

"Ok, now I know you're back to normal. The kooky ideas are flowing again," Tommy says laughing.

We sit on the stern of *Kingfisher*, sipping tea, watching the ducks and swans squabbling over scraps of bread thrown in by an old lady up by the bridge.

"Are you ready to come back to work? I've taken on your mate Steve in the St. Ives shop, but you could decide if you'd prefer to be there, or down at Marsh."

"To be honest I don't really fancy going back to Marsh Lakes. Can you give me a couple more weeks? And anyway, I'm not sure Harry would have me, he probably blames me for all that *FishAction* trouble."

"You come back when you're ready Kes. Harry hasn't said anything, in fact we've hardly seen him, seems to have lost his enthusiasm for Marsh Lakes."

"Not Harry's style to give up the fight," I say.

"No, but he's gutted, seems we lost most of the fish during the flood."

"I guessed as much, from the bivvies dotted along the river as I came back up."

"Should have fixed the fence immediately, but with the shock of it, the funeral and everything, didn't get around to it until it was too late."

This prompts another bout of silent staring.

"To be honest I'm desperate to get back on the Lagoon now, have another crack at the Lady."

"Fancy a few blanks eh?"

I smile. "It's all part of the experience isn't it? Just want to get behind the rods for a few weeks, see what I can winkle out."

And then Tommy's face lights up. "Ok, try this one for size. How about I ask Harry if he'll pay you to catch his carp back from the river?"

I sit there staring blankly at Tommy. Well it's not a bad idea, scouring the river for foreign legionnaires, but my mind was set on the Lagoon. Could I do both? Before I say anything Tommy is on his phone, pitching the idea to Harry. I can tell it's a goer, as they quickly get round to numbers. Tommy puts his hand over the phone.

"Harry wants to know how much you'll charge for each fish?"

"Tommy, I haven't even said yes yet!"

"Of course you have. This is Christmas, birthday and a quickie on the local bike all rolled into one."

"Alright, alright, I'll do it. Tell Harry I'll get back to him with a price later."

Tommy clicks his mobile shut, looking very pleased with himself. "Leave it to your uncle Tommy to sort you out the best bloody job in England."

"Thought you said Harry wasn't interested in the lakes."

"Of course he is, just mad it went tits up. You know he's a big kid. He's in trouble, someone nicked his sweets, and he's having a monster sulk."

"And you're the daddy sorting out all our problems," I say smiling.

"That's me, here to help!"

"Helps you too of course!"

"Oh let me think, hadn't crossed my mind that all the bloody work at Marsh was down the tubes without the fish!" We laugh.

"How am I ever gonna catch the Lady at this rate? I reckon you're trying to keep me off there so you can have her?"

"Damn, is it that obvious? You don't have to fish the river seven days a week."

"No I suppose not."

"You can take a busman's holiday, get on there on your days off."

"C'mon! Fancy a pint? To celebrate my new job," I ask.

"Now that does sound good, but it's only 8.45 in the morning."

"Ah yeah, of course. How about drinks at high noon, in the Ollie Cromwell?"

"You're on!"

I spend the rest of the morning sorting my tackle, just generally fiddling about with all my lovely carp catching paraphernalia. There's something very satisfying about a tidy tackle box. It speaks of a fresh start, renewed hope and confidence. But no matter how hard I try to keep it spick and span, after a few sessions, it's full of grass, dust, and bits of unrecognisable debris. I cut up old rigs, discarding any less than sticky sharp hooks, and set about filling my Korda box with eight inch size 6 combi-link rigs. Nothing complicated just a basic rig that will do the business and cover most situations the river will throw at me. I also tie a few of my floating hook rigs for the Lagoon. It worked once, so got to be the one for a couple of rods. By lunchtime I'm really prepared, how can I fail with such immaculate tackle?

My mind turns to bait. What to do about the mountain of bait I'll need for this river quest? The carp tend to be very nomadic on the river, so I should pick something that will hang around for a few days. This pretty much rules out my first idea, hemp and corn, the bream will polish that off in no time. I could go with maize, but for some reason I'm not a big fan of maize, a confidence thing I suppose. Ah, now I've got it, of course, tiger nuts. They're perfect, cheap, carp love them, they last for ages in the water, and very little else will eat them. I'll use my Monster Crab boilies tipped with a tiger as hookbaits, and possibly groundbait with some hemp when I'm actually fishing for a bit of added attraction. *Sorted!*

It occurs to me that although this is in many ways a dream job, if I'm not careful I'll be paying Harry for the privilege of catching his carp back. It's a novel experience, feeling like a proper businessman, pricing up a job, estimating materials and labour, calculating the profit margin. I need to figure out how much each one will cost me to capture and deliver to the back gate of Marsh Lakes. Questions flood my inexperienced brain. How long will it take to catch each carp, how many can I expect to catch, and how will I know if they are Harry's fish or not? The whole thing is probably illegal, so that's either a showstopper, or a bit of leverage for extra dosh, call it danger money. Blimey it's complicated! From previous experience on the river, I know you can wait for several days without any action at all, and then all hell breaks loose when the shoal arrives. Assuming they're shoaled up like their river cousins. They don't tend to swim past bait on the river, and dad and I have had two fish on at once on several occasions. Realistically, I'll be doing well to get three or four fish a week, but let's be optimistic and say five a week. So, at £50 per fish that would be £250. On top of that I need to add the cost of the bait, say £20 per fish, which would bring it up to £350 a week, not bad, but not great! Surely I could milk a bit more out of Harry, he's a multi-millionaire, and will pay a lot more for his monsters than the pasty's from the prize fishing lake. I need a sliding scale, something like:

Weight	Price
10-20lb	£50
20-30lb	£70
30-40lb	£100
40-50lb	£150
50-60lb	£250
60-70lb	£500
70-80lb	£750
80lbs+	£1000

Now that's more like it, a proper incentive for a bounty carper!

Whoops, 12.15, late as usual. Should be in the Ollie by now celebrating. I'm just locking the cabin door, when I hear the second familiar voice of the day.

"Hello *Kes*, where have you been, haven't seen you around for a few weeks? Nice haircut!"

"Oh hi Jay. Been out of circulation for a bit, up near Ely chillaxing on the river."

"Very sensible. Could do with a break myself, but things are moving fast with *FishAction*."

"Sorry Jay, not interested, taking a rain check on stress!"

"It's not more protests, if that's what you're thinking."

"Well that's something, I suppose"

"I've been talking to Jonathan Fox, the local MP. He's really interested in the issue, but wants to find some kind of middle line. I wanted to talk to you about it."

"Sounds a bit sly, can you trust him?"

"Good one Kes, he's a pretty straight guy."

"Didn't Tony Blair tell us that?" I say, smiling.

Jay hands me a folder. On the front cover in large print, it says Angling Green Paper.

"Why on earth do you want to talk to me?"

"Because, you've always got an opinion, and we need to canvass anglers. I want to check it out with a few people who know what they're talking about."

Jay's a smooth operator, buttering me up with compliments. "Just give me a quick summary, and please tell me it's not about banning angling."

"It's not, it's about regulating it."

"What about the ban?" I ask

"Well, it's off the agenda, for now."

"So what does regulation actually mean? Take Marsh Lakes for instance what would it mean for Harry's fishery?"

"It's not good news for places like Marsh Lakes, there'll be limits to stock density, tighter controls on imported fish, better fish registration systems, things like that."

"Blimey, you've been doing your homework. You sound like you now actually know a thing or two about fishing."

"Well you can't criticise something if you don't study it."

"You always were a bit of a boffin Jay, you may be cut out for this politics lark. Anyway the things you've mentioned so far sound ok, what else have you got?"

"A ban on keepnets and sacks"

"No mate, I don't think so. I'd have a problem if I caught the Lady in the middle of the night and there was no one around to take photos. I'd be gutted not being able to sack it. You'd have guys standing in the edge with fish in their nets all night, or just ignoring it. It's just not workable. And the match boys would have a fit about keepnets."

"And a ban on some hooks, what do you call them, barbed?"

"Bloody hell Jay, I thought you were going to say a ban on hooks. That would be a crafty stealth ban on angling, cos it's a bit tricky without a hook. A lot of anglers are unsure about barbed versus barbless. I think a barbed hook generally goes in and stays in, and worry that barbless hooks are more likely to move around during the fight and cause tears and scrapes. I couldn't prove it but that's my opinion."

"Ok great, anything else you think should be included?"

"Well one thing that pisses me off is people casting at fish that have just finished spawning. If I had my way, I'd make it compulsory to close any venue for two weeks from the moment the fish start spawning."

"Yeah, that sounds like a great idea, I'll email that one over to Jonathan too."

Wow, this is turning into quite a morning!

"So what does Saira make of all this?"

"Ah well, she's bloody furious, in fact, so disappointed with me, that she's moved off the *Heron*. Gone back to her mum's."

"She's not one for compromise is she, but she'll come round."

"Oh I don't think so, she's trying to get me kicked out of *FishAction*."

"That's nice, can she do that? I thought you started it."

"Well we started it together, but it's her latest battle. You know how she likes to have something to kick against. Suddenly I'm it, the establishment, and a sell-out all rolled into one."

Jay suddenly falters, and looks out over the river. I look at my watch. Tommy will be waiting for me.

"Oh well, welcome to the club. If you're not with her, you're against her!"

"Yeah, that's true."

"I'm sorry to hear it mate. Look I've got to go, I'm late, but how about getting together for a drink some time? We can catch up on bands and talk a bit more about this Green Paper thing."

"Yeah cool!" Jay says.

Twenty-Eight

When I look back at that period, I'm sure I must have been very close to the edge.
I'm not sure I even realised there was an outside world. I never read a paper,
watched TV or listened to a radio. I just went carp fishing.

Andy Little, 1992

t's not something I really think about, that you could actually fish too much. All say it together, we are carp fishing addicts! But it feels good and I love it, so what's the problem? Yeah I probably spend far too much time on it, but I do other things too, sometimes, in the winter, when the lakes are frozen over. Maybe having so much fishing right on the doorstep makes it different for me. I don't really have to make much of an effort to get the rods out. Fishing fits around other social activities, important stuff like music, girls and beer. Fortunately for me, work is fishing too. I reckon knowing what's going on in the world is over-rated, it's mostly bad news. I've had quite enough reality this year, and now I'm being consulted over bloody bills going through parliament. Leave me alone to get on with catching the Lady, and earning a crust catching tourists.

Sitting in Dave's point on the Lagoon, just looking, loaded barrow behind me, trying to decide where to fish tonight. Squeezing in a session before launching the river mission. Considering the weather we've had this year, conditions are great, sunny intervals, with a nice southerly blowing up the lake. Binoculars out, scanning for shows off the island. Where the hell are they? Could be right on the end of this new wind. At the moment the beach is free, and so is the bay. Won't last all day though, some chancer will get in there, so I'm poised for a quick move. Hang on who's that? Oh no, someone's coming down the slope towards the bay. Phew, not an angler though, looks like a woman walking a dog. A quick focus, Saira bloody Parsons. What the hell is she doing walking round the Lagoon? Must be trouble! At least she's alone by the looks of it.

She hasn't seen me, lurking in the bushes. "Oi, you know you're trespassing."

"Bullshit, I can walk where I like, freedom to roam!"

"I think you'll find it's called *right to roam*, and it doesn't mean you can go wherever you like."

"Alright smarty pants, what are you going to do about it?"

"Nothing, I'm just hoping this isn't you scoping for one of your demos."

"That's for me to know and you to find out."

"SOS, same old shit eh!"

"We're not giving up if that's what you're hoping."

"No, can't have yin without the yang I suppose!"

"What are you going on about now?"

"You know, chinese philosophy, opposite forces are interconnected and give rise to each other."

"You're a total space cadet aren't you Kes!"

"Just like ideas that's all."

"But don't take any of them too seriously, right?"

"Of course not, I'll leave serious to you. So what's next on Saira's list of big issues?"

"Live baiting. It's disgusting. We're doing a winter campaign against it."

"Well, it's not something I'm into."

"I should bloody hope not!"

"Nice dog," I say changing the subject.

"Cute isn't he. I got him from the animal shelter. I'm working there now."

"Yeah, he's great," I say kneeling down, letting the little black terrier jump up and lick me. "Wouldn't mind a dog myself."

"You should come up and have a look, we've got loads."

"Yeah, I might do that. I'll bring some hankies, I'm a big softie when it comes to dogs."

"It is heart breaking, especially when they've been abused."

"Bet you love working up there."

"I do, it's brilliant. I nearly didn't recognise you just then with that new haircut. What's happened to the head banger look?"

"Just fancied a change."

"You look like your dad. It suits you."

"Thanks."

"How are you doing anyway, haven't seen your boat around for a while?" Saira asks.

"I'm ok, just been away, chilling out. It's been a stressful year."

"Of course, wouldn't mind a holiday myself."

Just then a fish crashes, close. I rush down to my rods for a better look. Spreading waves 30yds out. Cast lined up. It was a proper lump. Then a real treat, the culprit, a big common head and shoulders again right on the same spot. They're here, on the back of the wind. No need to move, a night in Dave's for me.

"Wow, that was amazing. It was huge and golden," Saira says.

"Yeah, was a nice fish. Now I need to get a bait in the water."

"Swim away Mr Carp, you're in danger!" Saira says.

I laugh. "Not that much danger, I've only caught one this year."

"Let's hope your luck doesn't change. Anyway, I'm off!"

"Alright, see you around."

"Don't forget to come up to see the dogs."

"Have you got any Jack Russell's, or a black Staffordshire?"

"I had you down as more of a Poodle boy."

"Like to have the last dig don't you."

"Yes," she says, smiling, heading off up towards the Lawns.

With Saira gone, I focus on not buggering up this rare chance. Don't want to spook them with loads of splashing and lines everywhere. Decide to give it an hour with a bag on one rod, see what happens. Dave's is one of the easier swims to fish, with a nice little drop off just where the fish showed, clear to the left in the deep water and weedy to the right. Tiger nut tipped Monster Crab, a few crushed nuts and crumbed boilies in the bag. A flick of the rod, feel the lead down. Tell tale donk says I'm fishing, time to sit back, watch and hope. The minutes tick by, doubts build, expectation fades away. Confidence is never high on the Lagoon. They feel like super fish, who can spot my crude attempts to outwit them at a 100m. I imagine them swimming around in circles laughing at my rig, brushing up against my ever so obvious main line, flicking it with their tails to give me the odd indication. Taking the piss!

"Anything doing?" It's Tommy with his barrow.

"Saw a nice common an hour ago. Looks like they're on the back of the wind."

"Thought they might be. Let me guess, on the drop off?"

"How did you know?"

"Been putting a bit of bait on that spot."

"Great, now I'm poaching again!"

"No, you're alright, it's only poaching if you know. If you don't, it's good angling."

"Nah mate, I can't sit here reaping your harvest. I won't enjoy it."

"Look, how about this, we double up? One rod each on the spot, and both chuck another in the margin."

"I'm happy with that if you are," I say.

"Yeah, bit of a social and on the fish too, sounds good."

Tommy sets up his bivvy to the right of mine. I'm fishing in the deeper water, Tommy is happy to take the top of the slope and put one round the corner on a *little area he knows* in the weed. From the way he approaches it, I can tell it's another one he's been working, and where his right-hand rod would have gone anyway. Tommy is one of those guys who does it very quietly, no big fuss, just going about his business, watching and working the spots, quite happy to take on the fish and the anglers. No dramas and top rod or close to it, year after year on every water he fishes. When you watch him, you can't help but be impressed by the precision, the rods look immaculate, but this isn't a tackle tart image thing. He certainly doesn't go in for having his reel handles folded up. Not like me, I love all that. Someone in the shop was having a moan about us *young 'uns* with our crazy setups, saying next thing we'd have our reels in the boxes underneath our rods. So we had to get them out and attach them to the rods every time we got a run. That way we could get our rods practically touching.

Anyway, where was I? Oh yeah, with Tommy it just reflects his attention to detail. *Percentages Kes*, he says, if you give maximum effort on every part of the puzzle you'll find the solution quicker and more often than sloppy and lazy anglers. Of course he's right, but I can't quite summon the discipline. He's an absolute wizard with the marker float, finds spots other anglers just can't. And his hookbait is nearly always a 100%. Tommy hardly ever finds he's not been fishing the next morning. Not like me, if it's tricky I'll resort to the safety net of a bag or stick. Tommy reckons the fish can detect the PVA and are very wary of this tactic on pressured waters. I'd rather take that risk and know I'm fishing, than cast out a rig that could have tangled or got snagged up on a bit of weed.

"What have you go to eat?" I ask Tommy.

"Lamb Rogan Josh, pilau rice, and a nice drop of Chianti."

"A Silence of the lambs tea!"

"I like it, I like it, you're back on top form!"

"It's curry all round, cos I've got chicken pasanda with nan bread, Pukka! I'll cook it up on the Safari Chef. You sit back and relax."

"Don't mind if I do," Tommy says, pouring himself a large glass of red. "Do you want some?"

"God no, wine tastes like vinegar to me, I'll stick with the Speckled Hen."

We tuck into our spicy feast as the sun goes down, watching the water and a spectacular flame red fenland sky. Another show, further out, keeps our confidence buoyed. Alcohol, curry and a rod in the water, happy days!

"How's Steve getting on in the shop?" I ask.

"Yeah, fine, just a nutty as you, doesn't stop talking."

"And dancing!"

"Yeah what's all that about?"

"No idea. Thinks he's Bez from the Happy Mondays."

Tommy shakes his head. "You lads are getting crazier every year."

"Listen to yourself, you're sounding more and more like Ron."

"Poor old Ron, it's not the same without him is it? The world's turned upside down since this time last year."

"Yeah but I'm not looking back anymore, too depressing. Tomorrow, I'm off down the river and the start of a new adventure."

"I hope you haul, big time. I'm treading water at the moment. Got a load of stock sitting over at Marsh Lakes, and St. Ives is only just paying the bills and wages."

"Things have got to look up soon."

"Yeah, and wouldn't mind a bite from her Ladyship," Tommy says, getting up to adjust his left-hand bobbin, "she's the only fish in the lake I haven't caught."

"She doesn't fancy you. She likes younger men, Terry Hearn, James Brennan, Jamie Clossick. You're too old."

"Piss off. Here's a tenner says I get her before you do!" Tommy says.

"You're on!"

We spend the evening prattling on, enjoying the anticipation of a screaming buzzer interrupting our familiar carp chat. Eventually the wind dies away completely, leaving the Lagoon still and lifeless. Around eleven we've finally exhausted all topics and call it a day. Maybe something will happen once we're in our bags. Within minutes I can hear Tommy snoring, no doubt dreaming of a glorious start to the morning. I can't seem to sleep, too excited about being back on the Lagoon.

Twenty-Nine

A man is a success if he gets up in the morning and goes to bed at night and in between does what he wants to do.

Bob Dylan

adly it was the same old story. The fish drifted away, and the chance was gone. Tommy and I both chalked up another Lagoon blank. I was away by nine, heading off to Tesco for supplies. Am now cruising down to Earith, first morning on the job, my own boss. Time to locate some fish and start catching. I figure the carp are more likely to have gone downstream in the flood than upstream, so my plan is to do a couple of nights where the Ouse turns into the Old West river and the relief channel. There could be a few fish milling round at this point, and then I'll work back up to any good areas I've spotted and baited on the way down. It's a big stretch of water, and the fish could be miles from Marsh by now, but this feels like a proper challenge, and hopefully lucrative too. The river is now home to real pots of gold!

The pool just below Bluntisham lock is on my list of possible hotspots, and it looks like it's on someone else's too, because I can see a bivvy down to the left as I enter the lock. A blond lad is sitting at the entrance to his Trakker home.

"Oi Oi mate, you can't fish there, it's reserved!" I shout standing by the lock gates.

"Hello Kes, you're welcome to come and join me. No fish here at the moment."

"Sounds like a plan, two British record holders, we're bound to catch."

It's Steve, and I feel in the mood for a social, plenty of time for solitary confinement later.

"Can I bring her in just downstream of you?"

"Go for it, another feature in the water won't do any harm."

We secure *Kingfisher*, and pop inside for a quick brew.

"This is the life," Steve says, putting his bite alarm receiver on the table, reclining with a fresh brew and a chocolate Hobnob.

"Not too shabby is it!" I say.

"You used to be a right bivvy tramp Kes, now look at you, the river fisher king."

"Still am, but I can bring my house with me on the river."

"Pukka mate, you've got it made."

"So what brings the British record holder to Bluntisham?" I ask.

"Sounds good doesn't it? British record holder."

"Yeah even if it was a foreign tourist," I reply.

"Fair point! Anyway, everyone's talking about how the river will be throwing up some special lumps for the rest of the year."

"So we're both on an autumn river mission!" I say.

"I thought you weren't too keen on these foreigners. Expected you to be back on the Lagoon after her ladyship"

"I am, but in between I've been tempted by another job for Harry."

I tell Steve all about it, washed down with more tea and biscuits. He's keen to know what I'm getting paid but decide to keep that to myself, just saying I'll be splashing out on new tackle this winter.

"Bloody hell, talk about reasons to be cheerful, 1, 2, 3, you jammy bugger. I'd almost give up my Fen Drayton ticket for a job like that."

Then I have an idea, I could sub-contract some of the work to Steve. I suppose you've got to let your mates in on the action too! Well, a few scraps off the table at least. We'll have to talk to Tommy, as it will mean both of his staff out of action for the autumn, but he needs the fish back too, and the sooner the better. We shake hands on a deal that gives Steve 50% of what I'm making on each capture. I don't tell him that though, just that I'll make a little bit on the side of the fish he brings home. Everyone's happy!

"Come on you beauties, make me some money," Steve whispers into his bite alarm receiver, "bit of added spice to our angling Kes me old mucker!"

"Right then, I better get outside and find three good spots, I say."

"Yeah, off you go, I'll stay here, have another brew and do quality control on these Hobnobs."

"No chance, they're rationed. I want you in the tender, dropping my rigs and bait on spots in the cabbages."

"Hang on, I don't remember anything about being your personal fishing slave in the contract."

"Read the small print!" I say, laughing.

With the rods out, it's time to kick back, drink more tea and chew the fat. Conversation revolves around recent events, but Steve is not one to dwell on the negative side of life, so we're quickly onto what we can do to spice up our river campaign. I tell him about the BivvyTramps site I was getting into before Marsh Lakes exploded and then imploded. We come up with loads of ideas for webcasts, things like favourite swims and how to fish them, strokes you can pull while everyone else is asleep, rumours you've heard, top five bivvy babes, most outrageous bait you've caught a carp on, and on and on. Steve suggests a piece on carp tattoos. Turns out he's a work of carp fishing art, and having the webcam and computer on the boat, we decide there's no time like the present.

"Right Steve, are you ready to rumble with the webcast?"

"No worries mate, where do you want me?"

"If you sit over there, the viewers can see the river in the background."

"Ready?"

"Sure. Will anyone be watching?"

"Probably not, I've only done a couple and that was weeks ago. I'll record it and stick it up for downloads. We'll do an intro and then you can take your top off and show us your ink."

"Sounds a bit dodgy, blokes looking at each others' tattoos."

"Didn't I tell you, it's the Gay Carpers Club."

"Piss-off, I'm not doing something like that."

"I'm only kidding you numpty. Let's do it and see how it goes. If it's crap we won't put it up."

"Hi everyone, the Bivvy Tramp is back! The last few weeks have been totally mad and sad. You've probably heard what went on down at Marsh Lakes. Tragically, we lost our brother of the angle Ron Simmons and most of the fish escaped in the floods. Frankly it's been a crap time, but I'm back now, and fishing for lumps on the Ouse. As you can see, the river is just about back to normal, although the banks are trashed, and full of other bivvy tramps. Everyone wants a piece of the action. Today we're joined by Steve Banks, the current British record holder, NOT! Give us a wave Steve, wrong 'uns don't count do they mate! Look at his little skinhead face, only joking Steve. Anyway he's a top geezer, and has taken the carp obsession to another level as we'll see in a minute."

"First off though, a quick rumble through the rumour mill and a peek at the latest edges in the Ouse valley. Probably the worst kept secret in the country is the unknown 60lb common in the Colne Valley. Can't say too much more, but it's in a water that everyone can access so it's gonna be the next big circuit fish. I'll be heading there myself at some point, deffo! And at the risk of getting serious, watch out for the new Angling Green Paper. You can check it out on the DEFRA website. Seriously, it's worth a read, and whether you support it or not, you gotta email your MPs about it, put fishing on the political map! Get up, stand up, stand up for your rights, an' all that! Ok, enough politics, check it out! This is the Kiddie! It's my new floating hook rig......"

"Right then possums, have you ever fancied a fishing tattoo? Well our main man Steve is going to show us what an *X-treme* carper looks like under his Carpworld t-shirt."

Steve takes off his shirt to reveal a back full of fishy flesh ink.

"Take a look at that lads, hardcore or what? Talk us through it Steve. Which was the first one?"

"Well I started with the big leaping mirror carp, with the motto *Carpe Diem* across the top."

"Pukka!"

"Then, chatting to my tattooist up in Wisbech, we came up with the idea to put a bankside scene on the bottom with a three-rod setup, Steve Neville alarms and a line going out to its mouth. It just kind of grew from there. I had a couple more carp on each arm and started putting the names of the waters I've fished round the base."

"What have you got on there so far!"

"Oh mostly local places, Fen Drayton, Ashmire, the Woolpack, Elstow and also Yateley."

"So what have you got planned next?"

"I've been drawing up some ideas for other bits of tackle, fancy an arm band made of hooks, and maybe a cross made of a bank stick and buzzer bar."

"That's Rad, give it up for the man! Well that's all for now you cyber carpers, we'll be back online when we get into these river lumps."

We're pretty pleased with our first webcast, and settle down in our bivvies dreaming of carp fishing fame. Unfortunately the day is quiet and the night doesn't bring the treasure we were hoping for, just long sleepless hours as Steve is plagued by one slab after another. Mercifully my tiger tipped boilies were left alone by the dustbin lids, but I still jumped up every time his buzzer squealed. Right now we're in the middle of that morning ritual, *should I stay or should I go now?* Me sitting on a bait bucket, Steve tucked up in his bag, both scanning the water for any encouragement on offer. A ghostly mist hangs across the valley, the river trundling gently from right to left, the occasional roach splashing at the surface.

"A total of eight bream equals zero pence for you, and a blank means precisely the same for me. This is a results business, and we've made a bad start to the season. What's plan B?"

"The same, we sit and wait for them to come to us. And meanwhile I boil up some of those tigers you've got," Steve says.

"I'm not sure, reckon we should head down to Earith."

"Let's give it a few more hours. And by the way, I was thinking during the night."

"Steady."

"Filming these fish and webcasting isn't such a good idea. Talk about setting yourself up."

"Yeah, you're probably right. Not sure how legal it is. Still reckon we should move though."

This is where I employ the Brian Clough dispute resolution strategy. We sit down, have another brew, discuss it for a few minutes and then decide I'm right. Sorted. By midday we're all packed up and ready to rumble. Bivvy Tramps United are ready for their next fixture, versus Earith Town Carp. My heart sinks on the approach to Earith, as the river is high and the meadows still flooded. More encouragingly though, there are one or two very tasty looking snags. I drift Kingfisher in alongside them, and we peer down into the murky depths. The river is a lot more coloured here than over near Ely. Nothing lurking high up. I steer over to the far bank, more hopeful as this next snag is catching the afternoon sun, and is surrounded by a big bed of lilies. They're past their best for the year, but still always a good refuge for the river carp.

Steve spots them first, tucked tight against the bank, in a small clear spot next to the main branch of the snag tree. Three carp basking lazily, blissfully unaware of our plans to press-gang them into commercial service back at Marsh Lakes.

"Oi Oi Kes, three little river pigs ahead! Are you feeling hungry?"

"Not by the hair of my chinny chin chin!" I say.

"We'll huff and we'll puff and nail the buggers with a bit of Korda Steel!"

We decide that before we offer them a tasty tiger nut tea, we'll try dropping a floater on their heads. The only fair way to decide who gets first dibs is a chivalrous game of paper, rock, scissors. It's all square at two each, and then Steve pulls out a sneaky rock in the deciding game, blunting my scissors and ending my first chance for a professional capture. I comfort myself with the thought that I'll get a piece of Steve's bounty.

We creep up to the snag, giggling like a couple of schoolboys, and every bit as excited as we would have been back then. If you're doing it right, you never get tired of the adrenalin buzz from creeping up on your carpy prey, watching them circle your bait, trembling as you wait. The fish are literally a few feet away, on the other side of a large branch from Steve. He pokes his rod out, rests the second eye from the tip on the branch, and lets the piece of bread crust drop slowly down onto the surface. Textbook stuff, Jack Hilton would have been proud of us, not a bit of line on the water, and no disturbance. I'm a few yards upstream, crouching. I can see the fish clearly and am poised for action with the net. There are three good fish sitting there, all 20s, two mirrors and a common. The plan is for Steve to hook it, jump over the branch, and then we'll do whatever it takes to get the fish in the net.

It works like a dream. They just can't resist the soft white Warburtons wonder bait. Gill covers start pumping, pectoral fins giving a few small flicks, edging round, aware something new and appealing has appeared. We came at the right time, these fish are in the mood for a munch. A slight disturbance on the surface signals action stations. One of the mirrors turns round and without hesitation noses up to the bread, opens his mouth and then it's gone in one quick slurp.

"Strike!" I hiss.

Steve sweeps back the rod, the line tightens and all hell breaks loose. Three large carp make hasty exits from their sunroom, two of them free to fight another day, a third tethered by Steve's 15lb Nash Bullet line. Not your conventional floater line, but providing welcome insurance in such a snaggy corner of Cambridgeshire.

"Try to keep it up high!" I shout.

"I bloody am!"

Unfortunately the fish was a bit quicker than Steve, and got his head down amongst the lily stems. All is not lost, just yet, as the lilies are quivering above the tethered fish.

"Time for a paddle!" I say.

"Too right, that's got to be about £35 sitting out there."

And £35 for me too I'm thinking. For some reason, probably over excitement, neither of us thought to put our waders on, so, being in possession of the net, I have the honour of getting wet. The water is cool but not freezing, the mud is deep and worrying.

"There goes that pair of trainers", I say, sinking up to my waist with the first step. The fish is still a further five yards out. This is going to be tricky.

"How the hell am I going to net it?"

"Just try following the line down, maybe you can get it moving."

This is always a delicate operation, pulling the line up out of the lilies without further spooking an already freaked-out fish. In my experience, a fish bolting at this point usually spells disaster in the form of either a straightened hook, or worse, snapped string. I approach the quivering lilies very cautiously, peering down between the decaying leaves. My Wychwood Polaroids reveal a trembling carp lodged about three feet down, fins erect, gills pumping. This is not a time for thrashing about with the net.

"I can see it, but can't get the net down to it," I say.

Steve thinks for a few seconds, and then asks "Is the line pretty much freed up to the point where the fish is?"

I look carefully into the water again. The line is quite slack in my hand, but I can see it trapped and wrapped round the base of a lily, just behind the fish. It looks tight to his mouth and this is the problem.

"I'm going to try releasing the line from the stem with the handle of the landing net.

When I shout, you haul it up to the surface," I say.

"Ok go for it!"

It's all over in a few frantic seconds. Steve, expert hauler that he is, not merely heaves when I shout, but also wades backwards. This extra pressure does the trick. The carp wallows briefly on the surface, trying to get some purchase with his tail fin, just enough time for me to thrust the net and lift with all my strength.

"Get in there, you beauty!" I scream.

Steve is doing a little victory dance, ignoring me losing the next challenge, which is extracting myself, the carp and my trainers from the muddy battleground.

"Give me a hand partner, I'm sinking here."

"You little drama queen, it's only a bit of mud!"

Steve dances away back on terra firma, while I feel around with my toes for Adidas footwear, missing in action. I take the net arms from the handle and secure the top by rolling it a few times, don't want to lose it now. "Ah found it!" I say, using the landing net pole to carefully extract my ruined trainer from the mud.

Once the fish is safely sacked up, we crack open richly deserved cold cans of Stella.

"Well done partner that was one hell of a netting job you did there!"

"Bivvy Tramps 1 Earith Carp 0!" I say.

"But what now? I say we fish on, and then deliver tomorrow. The fish are here!"

"True, but I'm not happy sacking it until tomorrow morning. That's like 15 hours or more."

"You're right, it's not really on is it. Let's get it moved as soon as," Steve says.

The plan is to get set for the night and then do a quick run with the fish in the car up to Marsh.

We both change into dry clothes, and then head over to the Bluntisham bank, Steve holding our precious cargo off the port side of the stern.

"Careful he doesn't get mangled by the prop." I say.

"Relax, he's fine."

With fish and boat secured we assess the options for the night ahead. Steve is keen to capitalise on his success and fish over to the snag and lilies. It's not a good idea to put too many lines across the river, so I go looking for another area. About a 100yds downstream a flood drain splits off from the main river. I nip down to have a quick lead about. "Bugger me!" Right there, a rod length out from the bank, is an absolutely stonking common rooting around in the margins. I race back up to the boat and grab a rod off the top. Steve notices me scrabbling through the bait bag.

"You've seen one haven't you."

"Got to be one of Harry's tourists, bring the net, it's a MONSTER chance!" I say frantically.

"Calm down, don't rush it."

He's right, the temptation is to sprint back up there and drop a bait right on its nose. But it's not the one, so crawling SAS-style on my belly, I position myself where I can see the beast. A few tigers flicked out at opportune moments create a monster snack, then the anxious wait for the right moment to drop in the rig. Steve joins me, and we lay there, our noses poking through the marginal grass, watching and waiting.

"Go on, now's your chance!" Steve says.

I poke the rod out and then with the bale arm open let the string slip slowly through my twitching fingers. I can see it sitting in about three feet of water, line and hooklink nicely camouflaged against the silty bottom, pinned flat by the flying backlead, fishing, 100%.

"Hope it likes tigers," I whisper.

"It'll love 'em."

The fish has drifted out, away from the bank, and looks to be moving into the main river away to our right. All sorts of doubt enter my head. How many times have I ruined great chances like this? A lot. Sometimes, no matter how careful you are you get the feeling the fish knows you are there. Is it vibrations, slight movements, or some unexplained sixth sense? Whatever the reason, more often than not, the chance fades away like the fish and you're left feeling totally useless and frustrated. But then very occasionally, you find a fish, even better two or more, in the margins for a crafty munch, and you just know you are going to catch. This is happy days, and by far the most exciting way to catch a carp. Please let this be one of those chances.

Five minutes pass, no sign of our scaly friend, could be halfway back to Bluntisham lock by now. Steve is unconcerned, head down on his arm, eyes closed, snoozing.

"Oi, you're bloody working here!" I say.

"Relax, you're wound up like a spring. Here have a pipe, it'll take the edge off those jangling nerves of yours."

"Nah, you're alright, I'm perfectly calm," I say, squeezing Steve's arm as hard as I can. "Can you feel any tension?"

"Ouch. Suit yourself." He says, laughing, lighting up and having a long deep puff. After a considerable time, he exhales, "what you need is some carp therapy. I thoroughly recommend it, cures all adverse effects of modern life."

"You're on the money there mate. That's exactly what I need, and here it comes!"

The big common has appeared without us seeing it coming, and apparently it's hungry. It goes straight down on a tiger, then onto the next. This is tiger nut bingo, only a matter of time before our number comes up.

"Come and get it you lovely big porker," Steve says softly, "we're gonna take you home to Harry! You're a very naughty girl. There's lots of food like this back at Marsh Lakes."

"Shut up you plonker, you make me sound normal!" I whisper.

"Believe me it helps, I always talk to the carp when I'm stalking them."

"I've never heard Terry Hearn or Jim Shelley mention it!"

"Oh trust me, they do it, it's top secret. I shouldn't really be doing it in your presence, but hey we're partners."

And with that the line tightens up, we're in!

"See, they can't resist a bit of sweet talking, and a lovely tea time tiger nut," Steve says, laughing like a maniac and already in the water up to his knees with the net.

The poor thing seems totally bemused by this rude interruption to her day, and for a few seconds just wallows tantalizingly in front of us. Steve is tempted to snaffle her up immediately, but before he can, she regains her composure and gives a big flick of that impressive paddle. This is a proper lump, and I can feel a huge weight through my right arm. She powers off to the right, ripping line from the clutch. Ten, 15, 20yds, no sign of stopping, heading off round the corner into the main river.

"Bloody hell mate, she's got some grunt," I say.

"Go on then, let's get after her."

Fortunately the margins to our right are shallow, and we wade and jump as fast as we can, trying to keep in contact, causing a huge commotion. The fish can be in no doubt we're after her. When we get to the main river, she's heading up towards the *Kingfisher*.

"At this rate, she'll be back at Marsh Lakes in no time," Steve jokes.

"At least we know she's not heading back to France," I say.

"Yeah, you should have turned left darlin', the North Sea is that way!"

I start to get some control in the deeper water out here, but she still has a few moves left, kiting out towards the snag tree where Steve is fishing. Suddenly Steve's alarm bursts into life.

"I don't believe it, I'm in," Steve shouts, dropping the net and rushing past me. Steve picks up his rod and leans into it. Nothing, but I can feel him tugging on my line.

"Did you back lead Steve?"

"Oh shit, no, I forgot in all the excitement."

"My fish has gone through your line, take your bail arm off."

This is bad, I can now feel Steve's rig dragging through the weed. It's like knitting out there, a right mess. Everything goes solid.

"Get the dinghy Steve, we'll have to go out after this one."

Steve takes the Kingfisher tender off the roof, and gets the electric outboard from under the stern floorboards. I hang on, hoping the fish is still attached. Once afloat, we pick our way slowly and carefully across the river, picking up the lines, trying to sort out the tangle.

"Oh no just what we need." Trundling down the river a couple of hundred yards away is another boat.

Our attention turns back to the job in hand. The fish has gone to ground, or just plain gone. I can't feel anything. Steve finds where my line has caught his, bites through the Nash Bullet line and hauls his rig in by hand, wrapping it quickly and expertly round his knuckles.

"She's still on!" I say, bending into the fish and feeling her shake free of the weed. She begins moving downstream slowly, less urgent than before, but still with enough force to tow the boat.

"Who needs an engine, when you've got 60lb of carp power."

"She's making us work for our money this one," I say, hanging on and hoping.

The cruiser is now bearing down on us, showing no sign of stopping. Steve waves frantically, trying to communicate our predicament, but they carry on.

"What the.....? Oi, can't you see what's going on here?" I shout, but they just wave and smile. I plunge my rod down into the water, hoping the fish keeps deep and away from their propeller. It's a horrible moment, just waiting for everything to go slack. Steve is going mad, shouting, swearing, and waving his arms around. I close my eyes, then open them again, the boat has passed, and I'm still connected.

"I could bloody sink that bastard boat," Steve says, eyes raging, veins bulging in his neck.

"Relax, you're wound up like a spring," I say, laughing.

Twenty yards down stream the fish surfaces, and rolls over. The first sign she is tiring. A few more short lunges and I can feel we've got her. Steve leans out over the edge with the net, and I draw the fish and boat closer together. She's wallowing around on the surface, and Steve scoops her up first time.

"Get in there, you beauty!" I shout.

"Well done mate, good angling, you the MAN!"

"How big do you reckon?" I ask.

"That's 60lb all day long. What's that worth, £400?"

"Yeah something like that" I say, knowing full well, its 500 smackeroonies in the bag.

Thirty

Life is what happens to you while you're busy making other plans.

John Lennon

Steve is lying in the back of my Passat, monitoring the makeshift carp transporter, constructed from a plastic cold water header tank, some old blankets, foam, and a pillow from Mum's airing cupboard. Despite a rather sodden boot, there is just enough water left to cover the fishes backs as we pull up outside Marsh Lakes.

"You need a lid for this thing," Steve says.

"You're right, the road is lot bumpier than I thought."

I get out of the car and hit the intercom.

"Yes?" Says Harry rather curtly.

"Special delivery mister, a couple of clonking big carp for you!"

"Kes, my man, good work, come in, I'll meet you down at the car park."

Tommy emerges from the Shop. "Hi Kes, what have you got for us?"

"Oh something you'll both be very pleased to see!"

Harry arrives, looking surprised to see Steve with me.

"It's alright Harry, Steve is helping me out. I need a hand moving these fish back. He's totally cool."

"Hello Steve, working night and day are we," Harry says with a hint of a smile, but straight enough to keep Steve guessing if he's welcome. "How is our British record holder, got any sponsorship deals yet?"

"Hello Mr Plant, none yet. We've got a right couple of belters for you in here."

"Subcontracting eh Kes, don't remember discussing that?"

"It just sort of happened, and I thought it would get the job done quicker." I say.

Harry looks at me stony faced. He has a way of making you feel like you just stole from his grandma.

"Just messing with you Kes, good idea, the sooner I get my fish back the better. Hope he's giving you a 50/50 share Steve."

Bugger, I should have seen that coming.

"I'm more than happy with the deal," Steve says, looking over at me.

"The lakes look great Harry, first time I've been down for a while," I say, anxious to move on.

"Yeah, they look good but they're missing a vital ingredient, fish!"

"Well let's get these two back in!" Tommy says.

Water trickles from the back of the car as I take the blankets off the top and gently part the sheets. The big common is sitting quietly in its sack. Hopefully the foam padding has protected it from any knocks and scrapes. All four of us slide the tank backwards and then plonk it down on the gravel as gently as we can manage. Harry and I haul out the common and carry it down to Monsters. Steve brings the mirror. Tommy nips in the shop for a weighsling, mat and scales. We stand around for a few minutes, giving the fish a chance to get some fresh oxygen into their systems.

"Right come on then, I can't stand it any longer, let's have that big one out," Harry says. The light is fading, but the fish still looks mighty impressive, a huge golden flank of scales reflecting every last photon of light at the end of this special September day.

Tommy and Harry's faces are beaming.

"Well done Kes, that's the big Spanish common. Cost me a bloody fortune that one. No need to weigh it, I know it's 63lb."

"Could have lost a bit in the river," I say.

"I'm not worried about a pound or two Kes, she'll be feasting on pellets and boilies from now on."

Harry and I slide the mat into the water and I lean forward to sink the front. The water comes up around the fish's gill covers, and the giant mouth starts extending and retracting. I slip the fish forward and hold it with both hands round the wrist of its tail. It feels strong, but I wait a few seconds as it struggles for freedom and then let it go. It is quickly gone from sight, straight down into the deep margins of Monsters Lake, back in its English home, but still a long way from the place it grew up.

Steve takes the mirror out of the sack and wrestles with it on the mat.

"Proper feisty this one."

"Couldn't say for sure that it's one of mine," Harry says, "would have to check the stock photos."

"It's a lovely fish," Tommy says. "Let's weigh it." Tommy hoists it up onto his scales and the dial spins round towards the 30lb mark. "Bad luck boys, 29lb 14oz."

Bugger, just missed out on an extra £30.

"Go on, I'm feeling generous, you can have your £100 for that one," Harry says.

Steve looks at me quizzically, but doesn't say anything. I've been rumbled. While Steve and Tommy take the mirror over to Willow Lake, Harry and I go up to the veranda of the shop.

"Come into my office Mr Waterman. Related to Dennis are you? Could do with a Minder myself," Harry says laughing at his own joke.

"No, don't think so Harry."

"So, how much do I owe you then? About £50."

I pull out my little chart of prices.

"Very organised aren't you? I don't need it written down, keep it all up here Kes," Harry says, pointing at his head. "See if I'm right, one at 63lb and one at 30lb, makes it, £600. Bloody hell, what was I thinking when I agreed to this?"

"The big ones are the prizes, it won't cost you that much to get the 20s and 30s back."

"Buying my own carp back, sticks in the throat. Anyway, I'm suing that groundwork company, they did a crap job on the bund."

I almost feel sorry for him, but that quickly fades when I see the wad of £20 notes he pulls from his jacket pocket. Harry notices my eyes widen.

"This is what it's all about Kes," he says sniffing the bundle and counting out 30 notes.

"Cheers Harry, we're having a night off but will be back on it in the morning."

"Out in St. Ives celebrating?"

"Something like that, and a trip to Tescos for supplies." I say waving our wages.

Harry looks at me, and then pauses.

"Have you seen anything of those *FishAction* buddies of yours?"

"Bumped into Jay the other day, haven't seen the others." I say, ignoring Harry's attempts to get a rise from me.

"Still waiting on the sentencing for that plonker who got himself shot."

Got himself shot, I like that, Harry blew his arse off at point blank range.

"Oh yeah, forgot that was hanging over you. What do you think'll happen?"

"My lawyers are on it. Got a few lines of defence up our sleeves, extreme provocation, trespassing, violent and threatening behaviour, that kind of thing."

"Well hope it works out. I hear Danny is back home, not able to sit down, but he'll live."

"Won't be seeing him round here again, that's for sure. What else have you heard?"

"Saira has split up from Jay. They've fallen out over this new Angling Green Paper."

"More bloody nonsense from the townies eh? What do you make of it? "

"Well, I don't know really. Some bits might be quite good, but I'm not too sure," I say vaguely.

"Oh yeah, what bits are they then?"

"Err, the bit about closing down a lake for a week once the fish have started spawning."

Harry doesn't say anything, just looks me straight in the eye, "any other bits?"

"Limiting stock density seems a reasonable idea."

Fortunately at that moment Tommy and Steve appear.

"Kes is just telling me how he wants to shut down Marsh Lakes, he's backing this new angling Green paper."

"Harry, I just said some bits of it might not be so bad."

Tommy and Steve are both looking at me, trying to gauge what's going on. Harry is sitting there looking calm and in control. I'm feeling distinctly uncomfortable, keen to change the subject.

"You're too easy Kes, no challenge at all. Definitely a bloody closet Bunnyhugger though," he says, laughing.

"He's alright, just a few boilies short of a kilo. Doesn't know his arse from his elbow half the time," Tommy says.

They have a good laugh at my expense. It's the first time I've been back since Ron died, and right now would be happy never to see the place again. I feel bad for Tommy, he needs it to be successful, but I can't help thinking he's made a mistake getting involved with Harry. Steve and I make our excuses, and head off down the A14 towards the bright lights of Bar Hill Tesco.

Steve is quiet in the car, but I'm so wrapped up in my thoughts about Harry, that I don't notice at first. "Look Steve, I'm sorry, I should have gone 50/50 with you on the deal."

"Oh it's all right, it was your gig, and you didn't have to let me in on it."

"Yeah, but I shouldn't have stitched you up. Look I'll give you exactly half, we're partners!" I reach inside my pocket and hand over the wad.

"Count this into half each," I say.

It feels awkward for a few minutes, but as we pull off the A14, we're soon chatting about what we need to buy, and congratulating each other on the day's captures.

Thirty-One

*Experience is not what happens to a man, it is what
a man does with what happens to him.*

Aldous Huxley

There's something comforting about St. Ives at night. Everywhere holds a memory. The little alleys where I snogged juicy fen girls, or failing that, had an urgent late night pee. The quay, where I spent teenage evenings, trying to pluck up courage to buy bottles of cider, and wrestling dangerously with my mates on the water's edge. The bus station, where I got beaten up by a group of lads from March, after chatting up the wrong juicy fen girl, and the war memorial, where we laid a wreath for dad last year.

The Royal Tavern is our chosen watering hole tonight, a pint of Adnams for me, and Stella for Steve, the lager lout. Leaning on the bar, I look around, nodding at the familiar faces. Friends of dad's, friends of mum's, school friends, music friends, a couple of customers from Tommy's. Over in the corner, a group of crustys and in the middle, holding forth on some subject or other, as usual, is Saira. I keep my eyes on her longer than I should, it's hard not to, but she doesn't look over, too busy arguing with one of the lads buzzing around her. On the wall behind her I notice the latest gig poster. The Bunnyhuggers are playing here again next week, with a couple of other bands. It's been months since Radiation played and Jethro is right on my case, but I'm not doing anything this side of Christmas. Got to get the rod hours in on the Lagoon when I'm not on the river.

Steve and I find a table about halfway down the pub and begin planning our next session. A pocket full of Harry's cash has sent our minds racing about how much we could make, certainly a good few grand each.

"What are you going to do with the money?" Steve asks.

"I don't know really, could do with a proper holiday. Might go to the south of France."

"Yeah, that sounds good. Never been abroad, haven't even got a passport."

"They don't like fen folk going abroad Steve, in case they see your webbed feet on the beach," I say.

"I don't know why you're laughing, you're just as much a fen boy as me!"

We clunk beers, and agree to a French fishing holiday, *fen folk in France!* Just as we're drinking to our new plans, I feel a tap on my shoulder.

"Hello Kes, how are you doing?" Saira asks.

"Err, yeah, fine," I say having another gulp of my beer, and suddenly feeling awkward and tongue-tied. I know Steve can't stand Saira. "You?"

"Bit fed up really. I don't know if you've heard, but Jay and me have split up."

"Yeah, Jay mentioned something, thought it was just a row though."

"Oh it was a row alright," she says, looking at Steve. "Can I have a word with you outside?"

I'm not sure what Saira can want from me in private, but I'm curious to find out. It's pretty nippy. I pull down the sleeves on my Carpworld hoodie. Saira wraps her cardigan and hugs herself with both arms.

"I was wondering if you'd do me a favour?"

"What, give up fishing?" I say, smiling.

"Yes of course, but you're not evolved enough yet are you?"

"Suppose I asked for that." But I can tell that for once Saira is not in the mood for a fight. She's staring at the ground, and when she looks at me, her eyes are full of tears.

"I've really hurt Jay, said some pretty horrible things. He won't speak to me."

"I'm not surprised, I hear you've chucked him out of *Fish Action*!"

"Yeah. We've fallen out over this bloody Angling Green Paper. He's taken it badly."

"Seemed alright when I saw him the other day."

"On the surface, but he's drinking himself silly every night."

"I don't see what I can do about that."

"Could you have a word with him, and you know, just keep an eye on him?"

"Why me?"

"He likes you, must be some kind of guitarists union thing, and you're on the river too."

"Look, I'll do what I can. Don't want the dozy bastard falling in, one person drowning was bad enough."

"Thanks Kes, here's my mobile number."

"Where is he tonight?"

"Down in the back bar on his own."

Saira goes back inside, leaving me thinking *what the ... did I do to deserve this?* I have a slurp of beer and briefly explain the situation to Steve.

Jay is sitting in the corner snug, slouched over, head resting against the table.

"Hello Jay, you alright?"

He lifts his head, raising one arm, struggling to focus on where the question has come from. Completely rat arsed, drool coming from the side of his mouth, face swollen, eyes red and glazed. In the background Kim Wild is singing Kids in America.

"We're the kids in East Anglia!" Jay sings, giggling, rolling around in his seat.

"Yeah, good one Jay. Had a few wine gums have we?" I say.

"Hello Kes, mate. Come and join me," he says, trying to get up, but crashing sideways into the table, knocking the rest of his pint over.

"Come on, let's get you outside for a bit of fresh air."

Steve lends me a hand, and we drag Jay up the pub, past Saira and out onto the High Street.

"What are we going to do with you?" I say.

"Show me the way to go home," Jay sings.

"Good idea, where are you moored?"

"Meadow," he slurs.

Ten minutes later, we finally get Jay aboard the *Heron,* and dump him into his bunk. He's out cold. I put him in the recovery position, and sit down on the edge of the bed. His guitar is leaning up against the bulkhead. I pick it up and play a few chords. Haven't played for a while, and it feels strange playing Jay's guitar again on board his boat. A lot has happened since I was last here talking about Ranters and avoiding questions about Marsh Lakes.

"Bloody hell, this is worse than your place," Steve says.

I look round, there are clothes, dishes, magazines and empty beer cans strewn everywhere. It certainly looks a familiar sight. But not one I associate with Jay. He's always been so together, full of energy, basically a clean cut kid. It was Saira who persuaded him to buy the boat and live the boho lifestyle. Poor bastard doesn't look like he's living the dream right now. He suddenly comes to and hauls himself up onto his elbow.

"Kes, you're a good mate," and turning his head deliberately towards Steve. "Thanks for helping me home. Help yourself to toast and tea. There are some beers somewhere."

"Nah, you're alright mate. You get some shut eye," I say.

"You can crash here if you want," Jay slurs.

I look at Steve, who shakes his head.

"Thanks Jay, but we've got to get back," I say.

Jay looks disappointed, but raises himself up further and looks at me seriously.

"Kes, will you play this gig next week? It's for the Angling Green Paper."

"I'll have to talk with the other guys. Maybe, we'll see. Haven't played for ages, and am a bit busy right now."

"So that's a definitely maybe," he says, slumping back down onto his pillow.

"We'll talk about it later."

But that is the end of the conversation. Jay is sparko! Steve and I turn out the lights, shut the cabin door and head back into town.

"You're not going to get involved with this gig are you?" Steve asks as we trudge over the bridge.

"Oh I don't know, probably not."

"I wouldn't, it'll cause you a load of grief with Harry. Don't upset him while he's crossing our palms with £20 notes."

"You're right, we've got carp to catch!"

"No sleep til Christmas! And then onto France!" Steve says enthusiastically.

"Sounds good doesn't it?"

"Like I've died and gone to carp fishing heaven!"

"The carp fishing gods were certainly smiling on us today!"

With our evening interrupted by good Samaritan duty I've only managed one pint, so driving back to Earith isn't a problem. The plan is to get a few hours shut eye and then chuck the rods out at first light. We're both stoked, anticipating what lumps lie ahead and setting ourselves ridiculous targets on how much we can make in 24 hours.

Back on board *Kingfisher*, it strikes me that it's only marginally tidier than the *Heron*. We left in a bit of a hurry, and dumped both sets of tackle wherever it landed. Despite my protests, Steve insists on having a pee off the stern, saying it's good luck, and let's the fish know we're onto them. He then picks his way through the clutter up to the bow bunk. I turn out the lights. It's been another full on day, pretty cool, but confusing. I've really got to stop fantasising about Saira, she's totally not the one, but bloody hell, she's a whole lotta woman! My mind drifts onto France and fitties. Shame we're not going in the summer, the further south we went the bigger the carp and the fewer clothes the girls would be wearing. A country stocked with huge carp and heavenly girls, even the president's wife is hot. Nice! Exactly what I need, getting away for a couple of months, fishing somewhere totally new. I don't want to fish some commercial lake though, that would be just like fishing Marsh. I fancy doing Cassien, or one of the big French rivers, somewhere a bit wild, somewhere *X-treme*.

"Hey Steve, where else in Europe do you fancy fishing?"

"Morocco!" He says firmly.

"That's not bloody Europe, that's Africa."

"Oh yeah. I was reading International Carper yesterday, it's doing some mint fish."

"Not so easy to get there in a car?"

"Why?"

"There's a bit of water in the way, called the Mediterranean Sea."

"Oh, well there must be ferries."

"I think we'll stick with France, see how we get on there first," I say.

"Not very *X-treme* are you," Steve says laughing.

"No not really," I say smiling to myself in the darkness, "French fish are alright, but you can't beat a proper old English lump can you?"

"Well a 50 from Cassien might do it."

"I'd rather have the big linear from Fen Drayton."

"You're such a home boy."

"Sod off, look who's talking, Mr Geography!"

"Going to be a bit crammed in your Passat."

I think for a nano second and blurt out. "We're not going in the Passat, I'm buying an *X-treme* Carper's tour bus. Let's check out Auto Trader in the morning."

"Yes, quite a day!" Steve says.

Thirty-Two

Wherever you're fishing and whatever you're fishing for, just make sure you enjoy yourself, it's the most important thing of all.

Terry Hearn, Still Searching, 2006

The next few weeks were a total carp fishing feast, scouring the river from Earith up to Huntingdon. The *Kingfisher* served us well, the perfect river carp base. In fact, it would have been a miserable slog without it. The weather was awful most of the time, cold and wet, with constant nagging northerlies chilling our bones. As the river quietened down and the days grew shorter, we took to fishing from six in the morning to ten at night. Having the boat on hand meant we could turn in for a few hours of quality sleep and get back on the rods in the morning, refreshed, ready to go hauling again. And boy did we haul! We've fished for a total of 29 days so far and managed 44 fish between us. The scores on the doors look like this:

	Kes	Steve	Total	Cash (£)
Doubles	9	8	17	850
Twenties	5	7	12	840
Thirties	4	3	7	700
Forties	1	1	2	300
Ffities	3	2	5	1250
Sixties	1	0	1	500
Seventies	0	0	0	0
TOTALS	23	21	44	£4440

I think it's fair to say we thought we'd be talking more than a couple of grand each by now. But we needed to bank a lot more Monster Lake escapees to send our bank balances soaring. So far it's been mostly doubles and 20s. I didn't really think about it that carefully when I did the deal with Harry. A few more minutes with a calculator would have made it clear this wasn't the licence to print money that it felt like. Still a great job though, and 44 fish is nowhere near the number that Harry reckons he's lost. With a fair wind behind us, literally, we might just about double our money by Christmas.

We had a horrible day up at Huntingdon yesterday, pouring rain, four degrees, 20mph northwesterly, huddled under a makeshift tarp on the stern. Things did not look promising, but we kept positive, necking tea, bacon sandwiches, and talking about balmy days in France. It was looking odds on for a blank, but just when we were thinking about packing up I had a belting run on the right-hand rod. It was on a spot under the road bridge, in ten feet of water, and turned out to be a very foreign looking 34lb common. Result! Once we had it safely installed in the Passat, Steve headed off to Marsh, and I chugged my way down river to the Boathaven. I say chugged, more like charged; the river was rising quickly again, transforming itself from a sleepy old donkey into a runaway mule. I took a couple of bends sideways, which in a narrowboat is quite an adrenalin rush. It really has been a terrible year for boating, and now the Ouse is showing its teeth again.

This morning the water is charging through and they've closed the river to navigation. The enforced break to hauling has prompted an uncharacteristic but much needed cleaning frenzy. Steve has taken two big bags of clothes to the launderette and I've been through a packet of kitchen wipes removing all manner of unappealing stains and spillages. All the tackle is inside our bivvies, set up on the grass next to the mooring in the main bowl of the marina, near the river entrance. We're not too bothered about the flood, in fact, we think the rain may actually do us a favour. Our theory being that any carp nearby will be heading, like us, straight for the sanctuary of the Boathaven. If we're lucky we can just set up and pick them off as they gather in front of us. Well, you've got to be optimistic!

St. Ives Boathaven is a cracking little carp venue. In the summer, week nights are the best time to target the fish. They love to get in and around the boats and you never quite know what is going to be on the end when your buzzer calls you to action. It's even more exciting today, with the prospect of a few monsters lurking around the pontoons. Could be a bit tricky keeping a 60-pounder under control around the scaffold poles and other snags. Still we have the option of boating out after them, so things should be cool. The boats are being taken out just now, so it's a little busy during the day, but there are quiet corners developing as the plastic gin palaces are put on their winter blocks. I've got my eyes on two areas, a little deep hole in the centre of the main bowl and a deep margin running along the bank near the river. We haven't seen any signs of fish as yet, so I'm not planning to fill it in with bait, just a good scattering of boilies plus a few tigers.

"Hey Kes!" shouts a voice behind me, as I emerge onto the rear deck. It's Jay bounding his way along the bank, skipping over puddles, one hand holding down the hood of his light blue cagoule.

"Oi, can you keep it down, we're trying to fish here."

"Whoops, sorry," he says, doing a comedy tiptoe for the last few strides.

"Nah, you're alright, we're not fishing til later."

"You look a bit more perky than the other night."

"Sorry about that, I've been in a bit of a state the last few weeks."

"We've all been there at some point Jay. Anyway, what's up? Do you want to come in?" I ask.

"No I can't stay, just popped by to tell you the great news. They're taking the Green Paper forward, looks like it may actually happen."

"That's cool mate, you'll be an MP before you know it."

"Actually, funny you should say that, I've been offered a job as a researcher for Jonathan."

"Blimey, we are in trouble, a Bunnyhugger in Westminster, working with Mr Foxy."

"I'm quite fired up about it, and very excited about working in the House of Commons."

"Sounds alright, if you like that sort of thing. You could moor the *Heron* on the Thames"

"Not a bad idea, I hadn't thought about moving the boat down there. You know I'm officially banned from *FishAction* now!*"

"More good news, you're having all the luck this week," I say.

"Ha ha, bastards voted me out, irreconcilable differences."

"So you and Saira haven't patched things up then?"

"No mate, that's pretty much dead in the water. I'm focusing on the new job and London. A change of scene will do me good."

"What about the *Heron*? Are you going to let Saira live on it while you're away?" I ask.

"No chance, that would give me brain damage. I'll commute down on the train for now."

"So is that the end of the *Bunnyhuggers*?"

"Sort of, we're turning ourselves into a Smiths tribute band."

"Oh bloody hell, you don't half have some bad ideas Jay."

"I'm serious! The rest of the boys were never much into the Bunnyhugger thing, and I've had a belly full of it," Jay says.

"A belly full of bunny, sounds tasty" I say laughing, "given up the lettuce diet too?"

"No mate, meat is still murder."

"There you go, *Meat is murder*, that would be a great name for a Smiths tribute band."

"I think you're right. I like it."

I offer Jay a cup of coffee and a bacon sandwich. I'm cruel like that. But just as I do, he notices Steve plodding up the path with our washing. Jay is wary of Steve, and Steve does nothing to put him at ease, taking the bags onto the *Kingfisher* without a word.

"Has he gone?" Steve asks as I go below.

"Course he has, you didn't exactly make him feel welcome."

"Well he's not, it was his bastard boat Ron was trying to save when he drowned."

Steve's right, but it wasn't planned. Jay walks round ants, he wasn't planning to kill anyone. We stuff our washing into the bulkhead lockers in silence.

"Hey, I nearly forgot, I saw a VW Caravelle for sale in town. Here, I took the number down."

"Cool. How old and how much?"

"I think it was 2001, and they want £3,500."

"Sounds alright, we should go and take a look," I say.

I give the number a ring and arrange to go right over. The guy works in the small computer shop on Bridge Street, which is only a five minute walk from the Boathaven. Steve and I get into our waterproofs, head out along the new flood bank and then down London Road. It's the middle of the day, but the cars coming over the by-pass have their lights on. The rain drives into our faces, more of a straight ahead northerly today. Not good. We stop on the causeway for a giggle at any cars stuck in the Dolphin car park. There's always some poor bugger who doesn't realise it floods and comes back to find they've got a motor full of river. Even better if you catch them standing at the edge of the new lake, scratching their heads and fretting over a precious stereo, and best of all if they wade out in their suits and try to push it out. It's practically a spectator sport for us locals, and another small benefit of global warming. Today there's a bumper haul for the river, four cars with dirty light brown water lapping around their doors. At least they can share the misery, but alas we're too early in the day to catch the main cabaret.

The chap in the computer shop is sporting standard issue cyber geek black T-shirt, black Jeans, black Doctor Martens and pony tail. We instantly like him! The van is pukka, silver, what more can I say? Could only have been topped by matt black or camo paint job, which was a little too much to hope for. 90,000 miles on the clock, which Steve assures me is just about run in. Steve and I take furtive looks at our AA guide to buying a second-hand vehicle on the iPhone, wandering round tapping here and there, looking carefully at who knows what. We start it up, listen to, well, an engine sound, and take a spin round the block with our new mate James. We're sold on it, and being men of action, Steve happily hands me his wedge, a cool grand, and I dig out an envelope stuffed full of fishing wages. We shake on the deal at £3200, and drive *The Lady*, our newly christened European tour bus back to the Boathaven.

"Hey hey Stephen, I does believe we is sorted, broke again but ready to rock and roll our way down through France."

"Time to get those rods back in the water, we need a lump or ten to buy some Euros," says Steve.

"We'll see what we can winkle out of the Boathaven, and I'll post the Passat on *ebay*. With that classy camo paint job, it must be worth a few hundred quid. I'll offer to sign it too!"

Thirty-Three

My heart gave another lift as I realised it was not only gigantic, it was also a
beautiful specimen, sleek and bright, richly coloured – purple, ochre, chestnut,
amber. After all these years, all those lost fish, my line finally led to this great
mirror carp. We lay it reverently on the grass and stared at it.

Chris Yates, Casting at The Sun, 1986

Bivvied up side by side, rods out on the new Boathaven spots, chilli con carne on our laps, bottle of Old Speckled Hen for me, more Stella for Steve. Sorted! We've decided to do the night, maximising our rod hours and avoiding the boat removal disturbance. Fishing new spots always produces a great feeling of anticipation, and tonight we're fuelled by the added excitement of our new purchase in the car park. Thankfully the rain and wind have relented, and it's now just a damp northerly November breeze, cool but not freezing. Everything is set for a hungry carp to nail itself on my size 8 Nash Fang Twister. *Go ahead punk, eat steel and make my day!*

"Come on Kes, let's do one of those top five lists you used to do with Ron and Tommy in the shop!"

"Yeah alright, haven't done one of those for a while. Got any ideas?"

"I dunno, how about top five foreign carp venues?"

"How would we know that, we've never fished abroad," I say.

"Well, we know a few of the French waters, Cassien, Rainbow, Orient. Anyway speak for yourself, I fished in Yorkshire once, that's a foreign country to me," Steve says laughing.

"Good one. And of course Lake Raduta looks pretty special, but I wouldn't really have a clue how to rank them."

"Ok fair point, we should have a trawl through all those old Carpworlds you bought at the boot sale, check out which French venues we want to visit. How about Chantecoq?

That place looks awesome!" Steve says.

"Not in January, we'll have to head right down south to find any decent weather."

"Morocco?" Steve asks hopefully.

"Only if it's snowing at Cassien."

"I'll be praying for snow."

OK, how about this, top five UK venues you'd like to fish?" I say.

"Most excellent dude!" Steve says taking a long sup on his Stella, and gazing thoughtfully at the dark clouds drifting across the evening sky.

"So what would be your dream ticket then?" I ask.

"We're spoilt for choice really aren't we, but I'd have to say Fen Drayton, or Wraysbury, or Sonning, somewhere big, inland seas with proper wild carp, places you have to wean them off the naturals to get a bite," Steve says.

"So that's your top three is it? You need two more."

"I think I'd put Burghfield on there, just for the monster common, and I suppose it would have been Conningbrook or the Car Park at Yateley, but with Two-Tone and Heather gone, might have to go for Elstow or the new Colne Valley lake everyone is not supposed to be talking about."

"The first rule of fight club is never mention fight club."

"You got it. How about you?"

"Oh well I'd stick the Fjords in there, and the Woolpack, anywhere with proper old English lumps. Not very original, and makes me sound like a right local yokel."

"Quality lakes, quality fish, good enough for Terry Hearn and Dave Lane to bother!" Steve says.

"And the northern boys wouldn't be wearing out tyres on the A1 if they weren't."

"We could do a top five northerner and top five southerner list."

"Can you imagine the chaos that would cause on the forums. Anyway where does the north start? The Londoners probably think we live up north here in St. Ives," I say.

"True, we'll park that one. So where are you going to target when we get back from France?"

"I don't know, we'll be skint, so somewhere local. Might try for a Fen Drayton ticket. Seems mad having it on the doorstep and not giving it a crack."

"Good call mate. I can only think about one fish, that stonking big Burghfield common. Got to be done!" Steve says.

I sit there in the dark, feasting on the thought of cradling that beast of a fish, so perfect it almost seems ridiculous to imagine that Steve or I could catch it. Feels out of reach to mere mortals, a bit like the Lady. My mind soon turns to another favourite topic, a different kind of notch on my bedchair. "How about top five bivvy babes!"

"Now you is talking my man, got to be Cheryl Tweedy at number one, a little pocket-sized bivvy brunette, perfectly shaped for my bedchair."

"Bit of a Barbie doll boy are you? Not saying I'd kick her out if she forced her way in."

We have a good chuckle, enjoying the fantasy of the world's most beautiful women queuing up for a night in our bivvies.

"I know who you'd have on your list, that bloody nutter in the black bikini, Bunnyhugger girl, what's her face, Saira!"

"Yeah yeah very funny. Can you really imagine it? She's more likely to come and nick all your tackle in the middle of the night."

"Ooh blimey, sounds painful!"

"Yeah that tackle too probably," I say, wincing at the thought.

"Come on then who would you pick?"

"Oh I don't know, someone cool and interesting. Pixie Lott would be alright!"

"What's all this, would be alright, nonsense? Someone been putting bromide in your tea?"

"Girls, don't really mix with fishing do they?" I say.

"We're not bloody marrying them. We're talking pull up to the bumper baby, rock me all night long, I thought you were the rock star! You must be used to a bit of groupy action."

"I wish."

"Sure you don't want to do top five bivvy boys?" Steve asks. "*X-treme* carpers club, more like your gay carpers club."

"Ha ha, you just get funnier every time you open you open your mouth. " Idiot wind, blowin' every time you move your lips," I sing.

"Ooh get her, must have hit a raw nerve," Steve says laughing.

The banter is brought to a close by the sound of my left-hand buzzer registering a drop back. I jump up and hover over the rod, looking at the tip for any signs of movement.

"Could have been a liner," Steve says looking over my shoulder.

I look out to the spot and see some disturbance on the surface.

"I don't think so," I say picking up the rod and sweeping it back.

The rod arches over. "I'm in!" I shout.

"I can see that you plonker, I'm standing right beside you," he says laughing and reaching down for the net.

The fish moves slowly but steadily towards us down the left margin.

"It's heading for the entrance to the river."

"I can see that you plonker, I can feel it down my string!" I say.

"Alright, alright, caaaalm down!" Steve says in a very bad Liverpool accent.

I wind and pump furiously, trying to keep up the pressure and bring it out from the margin.

"How big do you reckon?" Steve asks.

"No idea. Every time I get in contact, it moves towards me again."

"Probably a pasty common," Steve says.

Once the fish reaches the river entrance I give it the butt, and she rolls over on the surface. In the gloom we can't quite see what it is, but the waves suggest it's no pasty common.

"Blimey, that looks decent!" Steve says, doing one of his trademark dances.

The fish doesn't do much, just plods away using its weight to full effect.

"Feels like I've got a dead cow on the end." I say.

"Hope not, Harry's not paying us for cows."

"Leave the jokes to me Steve, You do the dancing and netting."

It moves back towards the spot where I nailed it, but with a bit of pressure I coax her out into open water.

"Have you backleaded your rods this time? It's kiting right."

"Relax, everything's pinned down out there. Give it some welly, you're farting around with this one!"

"I'm not, honest. It's a lump."

The fish keeps deep, using its bulk rather than explosive power, but I'm in control now, and slowly shorten the line as it moves left and right about 15yds out. It's a great feeling when you have a fish in your sights. I put the butt into the top of my thigh and let the clutch do the work, applying side strain when needed and enjoy the moment, watching great boils in the black oily water and the curved silhouette of the rod against the night sky. Not too relaxed though, keeping focused, knowing it's also a dangerous time, when too much pressure can end in disaster as the hook pings out. I can feel there's not much fight left in the fish and start to exert more pressure, bringing her towards us from the right. She breaks surface and wallows around for a few seconds.

"Looks like a big mirror," Steve says, crouching down in front of me.

I walk backwards, and beaten, the fish slides towards the waiting net, mouth gulping at the air. Even in the dark it's clear I've bagged a very large mirror. Steve shines his head lamp down into the net.

We keep staring at it in the torchlight, moving it from side to side, trawling through our memories, matching up scales and body shape, disorientated by the location. It takes a few seconds for us to register what is lying quietly in the black mesh.

"Bloody hell, you know what you've bagged here don't you?"

"It can't be, can it?" I say, feeling confused.

"It is mate, you've gone and nailed the Lady! From the Boathaven!" Steve cries.

I can't speak, just sink down onto my knees, and wetting my hand in the margin, run my palm gently along her unmistakeable flanks, checking I'm not dreaming. I lie back on the grass, stare up into the night sky, and then slowly from deep down comes a huge wave of energy. "Monnnnssssster!" I shout.

"She's so luvverly, she's so luvverly," Steve sings, dancing away as usual.

"Scouting for girls!"

I jump up and down, then charge along the bank punching the air, I've got the Lady, I've got the LADY, the Fat Lady, she's mine! I'm not a camper now! Steve can tell my head is gone and suggests we sack her up for a few minutes. He grabs a couple more beers from the *Kingfisher* while I gather a few things together for the photos.

"Sorry mate they're all we've got, should be a bottle of the sparkling stuff really!"

I neck half the bottle, and throw my fist into the air again, saluting the carp gods for their glorious gift.

"Come on, let's get her on the scales and take a few shots," Steve says.

"Yeah, but hang on I want to ring Tommy. I'd like him to come and enjoy the moment."

"What about Harry? He'll want to be here. He's gonna pay big money for the Lady."

Steve's comment is shocking, and I instantly know what we have to do.

"No chance she's not going to Marsh. She's going back in the Lagoon."

"But that's several hundred quid's worth down there. And she's not in the Lagoon any more is she."

"Come on Steve, can you imagine the grief we'd get when it got out that we'd stuck the Lady in Harry Plant's Monsters Lake."

"Yeah I suppose so."

"This isn't a tourist, it's the Lady!"

By the time Tommy arrives, clutching a bottle of champagne and a tenner, all thoughts of cashing in on the great capture have been put aside. He's equally horrified at the thought of it, so the three of us enjoy a very special time with this most magnificent of carp, a real history fish. Even after handling some big old foreign lumps in recent weeks, this feels very special. She may be a fat old thing to some, but she's beautiful to our boggling eyes. Tommy and Steve seem really delighted at my good fortune, and I'm a grinning idiot in the pictures Tommy takes for me.

"So then boys, shall we get her on the scales?" Tommy asks.

"Does it sound mad if we don't weigh her," I say.

"Yes, of course it does!" Steve says.

"It sounds Kes, just like the sort of thing you would say," Tommy says.

"I know, I know. I just don't care what she weighs, and I don't want to reduce her to a number on a dial."

Steve makes a circle motion round his temple. Tommy nods and laughs. "Yeah, but it's up to Kes, he's in charge on this one."

"Cool, thanks guys, let's get her sacked back up and take her round to the Lagoon."

"Good job they mended that fence on there after the last flood," Tommy says.

"No more Harry Houdini's for the Lady then?" Steve says.

"No mate, she should be safe in there from now on."

"This is your last swim in the river baby. Time to go home for good," says Steve.

It's pretty late when we pull up in the Guided Bus car park. Steve can't resist, he stands on the rails and bellows out across the Lagoon "Layydeeeeeee!" Of course, it being November there are only a few hardy anglers left on the lake, but it's not long before a small gaggle of bivvy tramps are gathered round us on the beach. They can't quite believe the story we tell them, but it makes sense. No one has seen her for months, and it had of course been rumoured that she'd escaped. Tommy fields the "How big?" questions, saying we all decided that she wouldn't be weighed this time, just having her back was all that mattered. I stand in the water holding her, feeling her strength returning, enjoying my last moments with her. The chatter behind dies away, and we all watch reverently as the mighty back disappears from view. To my surprise someone says "three cheers" and they all join in, which chokes me up. All I can think to say is "that one's for Ron and dad," and look out across the lake towards the church spire.

"Absent friends!" Tommy says.

"Come on Steve let's get back and get the rods out!"

I say goodnight to Tommy, and make my way back to the car, stopping once to look back at the Lagoon. The car park lamps are glistening off the choppy water, and the lake is framed by wispy pinkish clouds against a black sky. This time it's my turn to feel a mixture of emotions, very happy to have caught and returned the big old girl, but sad knowing that I probably won't be fishing here again in the near future, not until the next generation of English lumps comes through. It's been a very strange Lagoon campaign for me, thirty nights, one carp and then the main target fish caught in another venue. That's Ouse valley fishing, you never can quite tell where the fish will be after the floods.

Thirty-Four

With a last lingering look I dragged myself away and as my little van
chugged up the grassy slope that led away from the pool I reflected on the
marvellous times we had enjoyed there, but which now seemed little more
than a dream. I reflected too, on how at times, we had been tired, weary,
lonely, wet and sometimes heartbroken, but always there had been the
awe inspiring feeling which just being at Redmire gives.

Jack Hilton, Quest for Carp, 1972

Christmas has come and gone, the days are getter longer, and buds are appearing on the Ouse valley trees. These first signs of life will encourage the Lagoon members. Once the ice melts, a few hardy souls will be back in their bivvies putting singles on likely spots, hoping for an early prize and maybe the ultimate prize, the Lady over 60lb in her winter colours. She's had a few months to settle back in with whichever of her mates are still in there. As I look out across the white crisp water meadows towards the Lagoon, it's comforting to know she's safe in her home, queen of the pond! Restored to her rightful place as one of the top target fish on the UK big carp scene.

Steve and I kept ourselves busy in the Boathaven, but the bites dried up around mid-December and since the turn of the year we've been concentrating on getting things sorted for the great fishing extravaganza ahead. Although we didn't haul in quite the way we'd hoped in those last few weeks, a further 19 fish still brought in just over a grand each. It was a great job while it lasted, but to be honest we're both pleased to have it behind us. Being bountyhunters sounds great, but the reality eats into your soul. You end up focusing on the numbers, looking for the next lump that will keep the cash coming. It's easy to lose sight of why you love doing it morning, noon and night. On the plus side, we had a great laugh, and are all set up for a month or two exploring the south of France for fishing heaven. What a year we've got planned, kicking off with a search for a wild euro monster, followed by a spring campaign on the Fjords, a quest for the Burghfield common over the summer and then back for the treasure in Fen Drayton during the Autumn.

We both fancy a more *X-treme* approach this year. It's got to be done. We're young and single, if we don't do it now, it'll never happen. So many whackers, so little time! We usually only focus on one water, but we're gonna fish to the max from now until Christmas. We've set ourselves a joint target of four 30s from four waters, a 40-pounder each, and one 50-pounder between us. Last year we were playing at being *X-treme* carpers, this year we'll be living the dream! No more crass commercialism. Having said that the tricky part will be financing a whole year in the bivvy. Might be back on the white bread, pasta and Bombay Bad Boy Pot Noodles. My plan is to rent out the *Kingfisher*, and try to get a couple of regular gigs. Steve reckons he'll get back on the Marsh Lakes bandwagon, turning up bleary-eyed and ragged straight from his swim! Good luck mate!

I can't wait to leave, it's bloody freezing here, with a northeasterly blowing in from Siberia. Inside, the log burner is roaring and the cabin feels warm and welcoming. Steve and I have tidied, scrubbed, hoovered, and wiped it back to something like its original condition after months of inhabitation by delinquent bivvy tramps. I'm expecting *Kingfisher's* temporary captain any minute. It's always dodgy leaving her uninhabited in the water in January and February, at the mercy of the floods and ice, so despite Steve's objections, I've gone for the boat sitter option. Passport, tickets and money are in my brand new Nash Zero Tolerance jacket, and the tour bus is fully loaded with carp catching kit. Thanks to Ben at the Boathaven, on the roof is a beaten up old aluminium boat that we've given the *X-treme* carping camo paint job, and in the back of the van we've got the pukka 40HP outboard, perfect for the grand lacs and colossal rivers we intend to explore. Steve has just nipped over to Huntingdon Tackle to get 50 kilos of *The Goodness* off Rob, and then we'll be ready.

Down at Marsh, Tommy and Harry are busy preparing for a first full and hopefully less troubled year. I said my goodbyes to Tommy yesterday, helping him move the last of the stock from the High Street out to the Marsh Lakes shop. It feels like the end of an era, because with the lease up for renewal, he's decided to close down Tommy's Tackle. I know it's only a shop, but I started going in there with dad when I was just a toddler, on my own as a funny little long-haired eight year old, as a cocky and probably very annoying teenager, and then as one of the staff. In one way or another it's been a part of my whole life. Not anymore though, and I've got to move on and find something else to fill the Tommy's Tackle-shaped hole in the world.

Oh crikey here comes the boat sitter. I scrabble around straightening cushions and curtains, and then clamber up onto the stern deck.

"Hello Kes, am I too early?" She says, black terrier straining at the leash.

"Hi Saira, no it's cool. Come in."

"I'll tie him up here."

"Is he boat trained?"

"Yeah, he only goes outside."

"You're a clever boy. You can live on my boat!"

"Wow you've really tidied the place up," she says as she comes down into the cabin.

"Yeah, it needed it."

"Well this is weird!" She says.

There's an awkward silence as we stand in the galley avoiding eye contact. I'm relieved when she asks if I could give her a hand getting her stuff on board.

"So do you want me to sign a contract?"

"No, it's only a couple of months," I say passing Saira's pink duvet down the hatch.

"Cool."

"Hang on, you won't claim squatters rights will you. After all you've got a bit of form on that front haven't you."

"No Kes I won't squat on your boat. Haven't given up the crap jokes for new year then?"

"I find life's so dull without them."

Saira rolls her eyes. "Are there any rules?"

"Not really, except look after her, oh yeah, and no *FishAction* meetings."

"Very funny."

"I'm serious!"

"Yes, I know, that's what's funny, and I mean funny peculiar, not funny ha ha, just in case you think I'm giving you any kind of encouragement."

"Well?"

"Alright, no meetings."

I hand the last of her bags down, and join her inside.

"Can I take that down?" She asks.

"What?"

"The picture of you with that ridiculously obese fish."

"Do you mind, that is the Lady, a national treasure, and the best moment of my life. But yes, I only left it there to wind you up."

She gives me a familiar loser sign on her forehead, but is smiling for once. It's a good job I'm going away, she's just too gorgeous and very dangerous for a bivvy tramp to know. Fortunately Steve arrives back at that moment, but stubbornly refuses to come aboard or acknowledge Saira's presence. He thinks I've totally lost the plot with this one, and maybe I have. I hand over the keys and we say our self-conscious goodbyes.

"Are you finished with her?" Steve asks, as I arrive back in the car park. "We're gonna miss the ferry at this rate!"

"I don't know why you're so wound up about it."

"Come on Kes, she'll probably sink the bloody thing. And I hope you didn't leave any tackle on there, cos it'll end up on the fire."

"She's not that mad. Unlike you, I like to give people a chance."

"Rubbish, you just fancy her. I admit she's pretty fit, but it's what's going inside her head that worries me."

"I can't help myself Steve. She just does it for me!"

"Right, quick, I'm taking you out of the country, you need some euro carp therapy!"

"You're right, let's get this tour started!"

"Take a look at this," Steve says, pulling up the sleeve on his jacket.

"Wow, that is wicked mate!"

On the inside of Steve's wrist is the *X-treme Carpers* mark, a black mirror.

"I had it done last week, been hiding it from you since then."

"You bastard, I really wish I'd had one done for the trip too!"

"We could maybe find a place in France!"

"No way, got to be done in Wisbech!" I say.

Yes, quite a day! I'm still in the front seat of the roller coaster, enduring and enjoying the ride, drinking nuclear strength coffee and trying to work out which way is up. I miss dad and Ron big time, and fear Tommy's taken a wrong turn, but everything that happened down at Marsh Lakes has just shown me what's really important. Who's interested in catching lumps from glorified garden ponds? Not me. I want a proper challenge, wild and intimidating, with a bit of mystery. You start desperate to catch one fish, then the most, or the biggest, and finally, you realise it's about catching the right fish in the right conditions. We pull out onto the A14, heading south, in search of *X-treme* European carp adventures. "Monnnnssssster!"

Carp: Short Session Success
by Julian Cundiff

Much-loved and respected angling writer Julian Cundiff's latest book is one from which anglers of all abilities cannot fail to learn, and whether you are new to the game and want a head start, or have been carping for years and want that extra motivation when times are hard, it's all in the 192 pages that make up *Carp – Short Session Success.*

Rod Hutchinson's Carp Inspirations
by Rod Hutchinson and friends

A must-have for any collector's bookshelf. At nearly 300 pages and over 90,000 words this is a big, big read about carp fishing by the men who helped shape its development from the minority pursuit of the 1950s to the global pursuit of today.

Just for the Record: The Quest for Two-Tone
by Lee Jackson

Compiled and edited by Angling Publications, *Just For The Record* is more than just a book about carp fishing, it's an important part of carp fishing history in that it documents the rise of this incredible water that once housed the much loved British record mirror carp.